BOOT
LANGUAGE

BOOT
LANGUAGE

A MEMOIR

VANYA ERICKSON

SHE WRITES PRESS

Published August 21, 2018
Printed in the United States of America
Print ISBN: 978-1-63152-465-3
E-ISBN: 978-1-63152-466-0
Library of Congress Control Number: 2018931069

For information, address:
She Writes Press
1563 Solano Ave #546
Berkeley, CA 94707

Interior design by Tabitha Lahr

She Writes Press is a division of SparkPoint Studio, LLC.

Names and identifying characteristics have been changed to protect the
privacy of certain individuals.

For my sisters and daughters.

The wound is the place where light enters you.
—Rumi

PROLOGUE

Spring, 1972

I ditched my math class, heading straight for the high school parking lot through the tall dry grass in back of the science wing. Funny how our community cared so much about the manicured lawn and flowerbeds and left the hidden stuff uncared for.

I slumped over onto the front seat of my ugly little car and waited to see if anybody had seen me. There were no footsteps or shouts telling me to get back to class. I slipped onto the road, unnoticed. I had to see Dad.

Glancing out the window as I drove along the old country road, I felt the land quiet my fears. The rolling hills were a green backdrop for acre upon acre of apricot blossoms lifting in the breeze, like party dresses. I wanted to be out there, to walk in the miracle of the land. But I had a job to do.

I accelerated through the beauty and connected with the freeway that took me into San Jose, speeding the last ten miles to the hospital, trying to keep pace with my careening thoughts. I hadn't seen Dad in months. Would he even want to see me? This thought was the rotting morsel I had chewed on all morning, ever since I had decided I needed to visit him in the detox unit at Valley Med. I finally brought my car to rest in the hospital's pockmarked parking lot.

I tried to imagine what lay inside the forbidding building that slumped in front of me like an aging beast. What did they do in all those rooms? Having been raised a Christian Scientist, I had never been to a doctor, let alone a hospital, except one time when I almost bled to death in my mother's lap when I was three days old. Mom betrayed her religious beliefs to bring me to the emergency room, her prayers floating above me like a halo. Though I no longer accompanied Mom to church, the teachings remained in my head like a dark stain. There was nothing I could do to remove it. Seeking medical help was an act of treason.

My older sister Margery had called in a panic the day before, urging me to go see Dad after he had been rushed to the hospital. She sounded breathless. "You really have to go—this may be it." I exhaled with the impact of her words.

I hated it when she prodded me to do things, but realizing this might be the last time I'd ever see him, I called the hospital, and a nurse informed me of his status. "He's pretty incoherent, dear." I knew there was more she wasn't saying. It was the way she paused before she said, "I'm afraid he can't come to the phone." I wanted to slap myself for being happy, but I was. I couldn't imagine having to speak to Dad. Not after all that had happened.

Now I was here. I sucked in my breath and pulled the keys from the ignition, looking down at what I was wearing. Was there a dress code for visiting your dad in detox? Oh, hell. My anti-war T-shirt and frayed bell-bottoms would have to do. I grabbed my macramé bag and got out. I threaded my way between the cars, the pitted asphalt heating up my sandals. I searched for the hospital entrance, my hair flowing out behind me like a wave from the force of my gait.

CHAPTER ONE

I was lying in a pool of my own blood. That's what they told me.

Throughout my childhood, the retelling of this story happened so often it became my bedtime story. There were three narrators: my mother, my grandfather, and the young woman who changed everything. I was too young to remember it, but this is what I imagine happened that day.

I was three days old, on the couch in my mother's lap, and she was trying to heal me. The storm outside howled as she squinted and leaned toward the lamp, the glow of the light softening her concentration. "Divine Love has always met and always will meet every human need." She was reading from her Christian Science manual, *Science and Health, with Key to the Scriptures*. Her head bobbed at important words. The slam of the door interrupted her words.

"*Buon giorno!*" It was the signature singsong greeting from our mother's helper Eugenia, a young woman from Italy my parents sponsored in 1953. She brushed the raindrops from her hair and entered the room, stopping midstride as she took us in: the tiny blue veins decorating my eyelids, my limp arms, the bloody diaper.

"*Signora! Perche sta sanguinando?*" She moved to pick me up.

My mother didn't answer. She just placed her left hand over the front of my diaper, as if to hold me in place. I can imagine her elegant fingers fanning out, covering my chest like a shield. Years later Eugenia told me that something in my mother's eyes reminded Eugenia of an old beggar woman back home in Monteleone, Italy, wandering through the rubble during the war, quietly lost to her own demons. Eugenia wanted to grab me into her arms and run into the street.

"*Guarda, la bambina!*" Eugenia pointed at me then clasped her hands at her chest.

My mother looked up at these words, her eyebrows one dark line. She had no time to explain what she was doing. How could she make Eugenia understand? Besides, she had a healing to do. She returned to her prayers.

The teenager's arms spoke in outraged jabs, pointing to the street. "*Prendi in ospedale immediatamente!*"

My mother lifted her hand off of my body at this outburst, and heard the teenager's sharp intake of breath as it mirrored her own and immediately placed her hand back onto my belly, camouflaging the blood with religious conviction. Her voice was louder now. "God is the light and the truth. Let neither fear or doubt overshadow your clear sense of calm trust. . ."

Eugenia ran to the phone, her index finger clawing the faded list of names and numbers on the wall. She knew my father was unreachable, so she dialed his father, my Grandpa Louie, who lived down the street.

She cried into the phone, "*La bambina e molto malata!*"

Although Grandpa Louie adored Italian opera, he did not understand her words, but they felt like a shattering of all that was good. He chased each syllable that leapt from her lips, comprehending the tone, understanding the terror.

Eugenia stood holding the door open as my grandfather peeled into the driveway minutes later. His long khaki legs rushed past her as he crossed the foyer onto the living room. "Margot! What's happened?"

My mother pursed her lips and lifted me to her shoulder. "Oh, I was just doing some thinking about. . . the bleeding." Her face tightened for having mentioned it. She shouldn't have said it aloud.

My grandfather saw the red smear on my blanket. "Jesus, Margot! Get in the car."

I like to imagine that Mom was relieved to follow orders, to allow my Grandpa Louie, whom she adored, to come to her rescue, for she said nothing and put up no fight. Grabbing her big black pocket book, she rushed to the car as if it had been her idea, but she didn't stop praying. She knew it didn't matter where she prayed. Healing could happen on the couch, in the front seat of the Pontiac, or at the hospital. God was everywhere.

We careened through the streets, Grandpa Louie's uneven foot on the gas punctuating the journey in nauseating bursts. Twice he reached his arm out at sudden stops to shield us. The rain had let up, but the streets were still wet and the late afternoon sun reflected off the bumpers, forcing my grandfather to squint. I know he was much younger when this happened, but when I replay the story in my mind, he is old and his too-tight grip on the steering wheel shakes. His lake blue eyes dart from me to the street, his thin white hair floating above, like a cloud.

Years later as a young child, I would play all alone in his Pontiac, hoping to remember something that would help me understand what had happened that day. I'd sit in the driver's seat and pretend to be Grandpa Louie. I'd scooch to the right and be Mom, praying. I'd lie down between these two spots on the soft bench seat, curling into a tight ball, a bleeding baby, my face looking up toward the ceiling of the old Pontiac.

When Grandpa Louie pulled into the parking lot of San Jose Hospital, he burst from the car and shepherded us through the entrance to the emergency room, shouting, "We got a three-day-old baby girl here!"

A nurse rushed forward, peeling the bloody blanket away. "It's her umbilical knot. Did you pick it?"

Mom refused to respond to this silly question. The nurse had never met a Christian Scientist before. She didn't know that they didn't believe doctors or that they saw the body as a kind of mirage, an illusion created by evil. And she certainly didn't know mentioning my symptoms could give evil more power. No wonder Mom didn't answer. She was protecting me.

Mom closed her eyes and softy chanted, "There is no life, truth, intelligence or substance in matter. . ."

"Ma'am?!" The word shot from the nurse's mouth, cutting the prayer short, as she grabbed me from my mother's arms and ran into the emergency room, my limp body, pressed to her chest.

Mom moved to a grey plastic chair, one of the many that lined the walls of the waiting room. She placed her pocket book on the seat next to her and reached inside, past the tissues and red lipstick, for her Bible. She didn't get up for water or food. She simply sat and prayed.

Grandpa Louie began to pace the glossy linoleum floors, his spidery legs taking him away from the sight of her. Finding a phone in the lobby, he called his son, my father, but he was in a meeting. Slamming the receiver down, he checked his watch: 5:00. He caught a glimpse of Mom with her head bent forward as he turned a corner and headed into the belly of the hospital.

Ten minutes later a doctor approached. "We don't have much time. Your daughter has lost a lot of blood and needs a transfusion." My mother looked confused, his words complicated, traveling from another world.

"Ma'am, do you hear me? Because of her massive blood loss, your daughter will have serious problems, most likely with her liver. There's also a good chance she will be retarded."

"Oh?" Mom was surprised the mention of retardation gripped her so. She looked up at him.

The doctor's smile was tight. "We have a donor who'd like to help. He's a new father, waiting for his child to be born upstairs. Do we have your permission?"

"Of course you have her permission!" My grandfather's shout came clear across the lobby. All heads turned in his direction. He had just completed another lap of the hallways. "Jesus, Margot, answer him!" Mom closed her eyes to my grandfather's roar. She mouthed a prayer.

The doctor nodded to the nurse at the desk, who was speaking to a tall black man, his face dipped toward the floor as he listened. They both looked over at Mom.

The nurse spoke softly as they walked forward. "Mrs. Erickson, this is Mr. Hamilton." She put her hand on the tall man's forearm. "He has your daughter's blood type. Will you let him help your baby?"

My mother looked up into his face and smiled. "Hello." She rose to her feet and offered him her hand. The heat of his touch rushed through her.

"Are you insane?" my grandfather shouted. "You can't put a nigger's blood in my granddaughter. What kind of a joint is this? You'll kill her!"

"Oh Louie, stop it!" Mom's voice surprised them all as she moved her body in front of Mr. Hamilton and stood to face my grandfather, hands on her hips. "Oh yes, she *will* have his blood."

And with this act of solidarity with her progressive politics, my mother bent her religious vows and saved my life.

―――――

This story affected everything, and was the birth of a great debate. Had my mother healed me? Or had the blood transfusion? It all depended on who was telling the story. But no matter the truth, I knew I was lucky. My earliest memory is of being four years old, lying on a blanket in the backyard of my home in Saratoga, California, looking up at the lush Santa Cruz Mountains, and marveling that I was alive.

I felt a deep connection with the Earth cradling my body, and if I could have, I would have burrowed into the earth like an animal. This rooted my tender love for everything. It was the small things that brought tears to my eyes: the dramatic calls of a mockingbird that perched on the chimney day after day; the long breath of the wind in the pine trees on a summer hike; the toothy smile of our retriever Brownie and the soft whop-whop of her tail against my leg when I came home from my best friend's house. I couldn't imagine a more magical life.

I can't pinpoint the exact day that things darkened, but it happened somewhere around my sixth birthday. One Saturday morning, the spring before first grade, my little sister KK and I were in our small TV room, when I heard Dad's voice. "Girls?"

Alarmed by the pitch of his voice, I jumped up from my perch in the warm bear-sized chair where I had been reading. KK looked up from her coloring, the blue crayon still in her grip.

"I just heard some serious news, kids." He appeared in the doorway, like a redwood, his gnarled boots the weathered trunk. As his breath slowed, one hand plucked a handkerchief from his pocket and dabbed at his neck. Had he been running?

Dad pushed out his lower lip and blew a blast of air toward his forehead, causing his baby-fine hair to float above his head, unmoored. "I am sorry to say kids, but the Boy Scouts found a pair of huge footprints right behind our house." I looked over at KK. "You sure you want to hear about this?" We didn't move.

Dad took three strides across the room and yanked open the curtains. "Look." He squinted, surveying the mountain, as if on a reconnaissance mission. Nodding his head as if pleased with what he saw, he tapped on the window twice with his index finger. "Right there. That's where they found them." He peered back at us.

I looked out the window, past his finger. Last night's downpour had made everything on the mountain seem magnified, almost within reach. Each tree in the emerald hillside stood out clearly from its neighbor. The earth felt reborn as the sunlight kissed the moisture from the leaves. Was it really possible to see the footprints from here?

Dad's voice dropped to a whisper. "Now don't be frightened, but this next part's pretty gruesome. It seems they were hiking and they came upon some fur stuck on a branch, long white shaggy wisps of it, not matching the fur of any animal that lives up there. They followed its trail for hours and hours, and just when they were about to turn around, at the muddiest part of their climb, they saw gigantic footprints at the base of a tree, like some creature had been standing there waiting for its next meal."

I closed my eyes, seeing it all as if I were there on the mountain, my nose filled with the perfume of wet earth and pines and wisps of fur.

"Now here's the most shocking part." Dad continued, "Experts believe it was—" Dad paused here as we looked up "—the Abominable Snowman." Dad face was all grimace, lips framing clenched teeth.

"What?" KK asked. She spat the word out. "Bom-able?"" Dad smiled. "Ab-bom-in-a-ble. He pronounced it slowly. "It means horrible. Terrible. A real live monster. Say it, girls."

KK and I repeated the mouthful of syllables over and over. Each time the sound of it forced our mouths open, like a stranger struggling to get out. Although I liked the newness of the word and the resulting jolt it sent through my body, I shuddered at what was waiting out there on the mountain.

"Now, don't you two go running off to investigate, or you just might end up on the menu. I'll let you know when the coast is clear." Dad nodded.

"How do they know it's the Abominable Snowman?" I could tell KK's mind was gathering facts as she tilted her head sideways and squinted up at Dad.

"Easy! The footprints were almost three times the size of a grown man's."

Dad thrust out his hands demonstrating the length. "Can you imagine seeing that on the trail? When all you've got is some lousy scout leader to protect you?"

I covered my face with my hands so I couldn't see him, now certain the creature was peering at us through the uncurtained window. Where had he come from? What did he want? Where was his family? Wait! What if he was lonely!

Dad and KK continued their discussion, but I had muffled their words with questions. What would they do if they found him? Would he be sent to the zoo where he'd live the rest of his life in a rusted cage like that old brown bear we saw at the county fair? Why did we have to capture him at all?

With a sudden whoosh, Dad pulled the curtain closed. "So remember girls, don't go wandering around out there. You're only safe when I say so."

After he left the room, I couldn't help but wonder. Had I imagined it or was he smiling when he left? Had he really meant I was going to have to ask his permission to go outside? I realized I'd be doing a lot of asking, since that's where I loved to play. Or was he just making stuff up to get us to do what he wanted? I shook my head in confusion. Adults were strange. You never knew what was really on their minds.

Later I asked my big brother Walt what he thought. I figured at twelve he knew a lot. He just laughed and shook his head. "Oh, man, I can't believe you fell for that! There's no such thing as an abominable snowman, you dope. He's just messing with you."

After that I wasn't sure whom to trust, and figured I had to follow my gut, but I always looked out at the mountain whenever I left the house, never completely able to get the abominable snowman out of my mind. Was it possible Walt was wrong? Maybe Dad really was trying to protect us.

One day in the fall of 1960, a couple months after the start of first grade, Dad swung his battered green toolbox onto my bed, right next to me. I had just come home from school and was still in my frilly school dress, plopped on the bed, thumbing through *The Cat in the Hat*. The hinges of the toolbox complained as Dad lifted the lid, a metallic question mark, like the pop of a wall furnace that made my head turn. What was Dad's toolbox doing on my bed?

Inside, a mismatched collection of rust-spotted tools lay like a sleeping family in two trays that looked like bunk beds. A mockingbird called from the rooftop as Dad searched the toolbox. He fingered a pair of needle-nosed pliers, the ones with red handle grips that made them look like they wore pants.

He looked at me, and smiled. "There are several kinds of pliers, and they each have a different use."

I tried to pay attention because sometimes his stories got exciting. As if setting out on a hike, his words were twists and turns on the trail, and I'd lean into the grit of his story as he led me deeper and deeper into the woods, until they got too scary and Mom would say, "Oh, Mack!" and I'd squeal and run from the room.

But now I couldn't concentrate. It hurt when I pushed my tongue against my front tooth for the hundredth time, but I couldn't stop. Dad continued talking, and I'd catch a word or two, but nothing anchored to my brain.

Earlier that morning, I'd felt my tooth wiggle and I'd run to Mom. What was happening? I'd found her in her "reading the Bible spot" sprawled across the bed in her red satin robe. She'd put a manicured finger on the page to hold her place, and looked at me. "We all lose teeth, honey."

"But why?" I didn't get it. But she didn't say anything more.

At school that day as I worked my tongue against it, my teacher put her hand on my shoulder. "The tooth fairy says it's not quite ready to come out yet, dear. In a few of days, your parents will know just what to do. They'll place a little bit of gauze over the tooth and twist it right out."

Gauze? That sounded like medicine to me, and my mom didn't believe in medicine. She believed in God. Would my tooth come out anyway?

"Open your mouth," Dad said now, bringing my attention back to the pliers again. I looked up at him as a lawn mower growled to life next door.

What did he just say? Dad stood facing me with the pliers in his hand, and it was as if someone had whooshed aside a curtain. I understood exactly what he was going to do, and time slowed down. Suddenly, I wasn't in my body. I was floating above, free and safe.

Why wouldn't he wait like my teacher said he would? I shook my head as if I could stop him, but opened my mouth.

"Wider," he said a little too loudly. Why was he angry? "You'll thank me later."

I didn't dare respond, just pressed two fingers against the pain, listening to Dad's retreating footsteps. I glanced at the tooth, weightless as a soap bubble, resting in my palm. Why had I told my teacher that my tooth hurt? It looked like the face of a miniature blood-smeared devil, a dark cobweb of tissue clinging to the side of it. I wiped it down, wrapped it in a tissue, and slipped it under my pillow. Would the tooth fairy still come?

The tooth fairy had indeed visited me, stealing away that bloodstained tooth. Mom was extra-specially nice, buying me a new Barbie outfit, the blue stewardess dress with high heels and cap. And the next night she took me clothes shopping. I was so caught up in the newness of things, within a week it was as if the tooth incident never happened.

A week later the whole family was gathered at the dinner table when Dad said, "Nobody make plans for next Saturday. We're going to check out the world famous Tree Circus in the Santa Cruz Mountains."

My brothers groaned. They hated outings with the whole family.

"Enough out of you birds. Listen to this!" Dad pushed back his chair and strode into the living room to grab *Life* magazine.

"Tree Circus?" KK asked when Dad left of the room.

"It's an oddity museum, honey, like Ripley's Believe It or Not in San Francisco. You might like it." Her words had a shadow of disapproval, but her smile appeared when Dad returned, flipping the pages of the magazine.

Dad seemed quite breathless as he read aloud to us. The article went on and on about a lot of boring things I didn't understand. I pretended to, though. I wanted to like this thing he wanted to see. Finally the story ended by saying that the creator of the museum never left the property for fear visitors wouldn't be able to view his trees. Dad's voice sounded reverent. What must that feel like to have created something so wonderful? I couldn't wait to get inside.

That Saturday, as planned, we all piled out of the car and headed for the entrance of the open-air museum.

"Will you look at that!" Dad's voice was so whispery soft it was a miracle that I even heard him. In front of us stood the Basket Tree, and at the sight of it I wanted to flee. It was a bunch of slender trees planted in a big circle and somehow woven together, with no limbs, until way up at the top, where it leafed out as if it were one big tree. At first glance, it looked like a tree without the insides of a trunk, more a cage than a tree, and it made my stomach lurch. Why would anybody do that to a tree?

Dad slowly walked around the Basket Tree, then got down on all fours, his eyes scanning the multiple trunks. He probed everything within reach, every place where the little trees interconnected, then he turned and faced us. "Well kids, they say Axel Erlandson got the trees into this shape by talking to them." Dad smiled and shook his head as if he knew better. "But I bet ol' Axel had some tricks up his sleeve. The man's a God-damned genius."

I looked over at Dad, my eyebrows scrunched together. I didn't think the guy who did all this to trees was a genius at all. I thought he was nuts. I looked back at the redwoods on the mountain. Normal trees—beautiful trees. I wanted to leave, but we had just arrived.

With names like The Bird Cage, The Phone Booth, and The Double Valentine, this Tree Circus featured dozens and dozens of trees forced to grow at disturbing angles and curves. At six years old, I was convinced that the trees were harmed in order to do this, and my theory was confirmed when I learned later that Axel had used wires, steel and knives in order to twist and distort the trees against their will, to change them into a bizarre idea of beauty.

I didn't want to look at them. I stepped away to investigate the birds in a tree when I heard Dad's voice. "Jesus H. Christ, come here!" I ran to his voice as he stood beneath the giant Tree with Two Legs, two trees planted far apart on opposite sides of a wide walking path. Yards above Dad's head the two trunks bent toward each other, connecting into one trunk. How was this possible?

"Yoo-hoo, Mack. . . look this way!" Mom snapped his picture. I felt dizzy. Suddenly Dad looked so small. His size made no sense, like he was the tree's little child. He even smiled like a toddler.

Later, when we were climbing back into the car I leaned my head against the window glass. I always sat directly behind Dad, and his cigarette smoke made an air trail to me. I wouldn't be allowed to open the window, because it bothered his ears, so I closed my eyes and breathed in the smoke.

Dad turned on the radio and began to sing along with Nat King Cole as he pulled onto the highway. "Pretend you're happy when you're blue. . ."

I didn't understand my father. All that forcing, cutting, and bending. Why couldn't the trees be left alone? Trees were born beautiful already.

CHAPTER TWO

By the time I was eight, I felt like an outsider. Was I even related to my parents? I'd ask questions about my past and theirs. Dad never shared anything, leaving Mom to her shorthand retellings of the most dramatic highlights: her mother's leap from their four-story flat when Mom was twenty; how Mom and Dad met in Manhattan during World War II as she entertained soldiers at the Stage Door Canteen; my near-death healing as a baby. But I wanted to know so much more. With the help of my persistent little sister KK, we were able to put stories together from casual things mentioned, things overheard, and the generous storytelling of our grandparents.

Mom was compassionate, musically talented, and although independently wealthy, searching for some deeper meaning to life other than social standing. A staunch supporter of the underdog, the arts, and liberal politics, she found her way to Christian Science not too long after she married my father.

Dad was of humbler stock, stoic and charming in his Naval dress-whites when they first met. But years later he returned war-worn, a staunch atheist. When Mom converted to Christian Science the sparks flew. He had no tolerance for her decision, believing his own mother, who was a devout Christian Scientist, had pushed her into it. And he blamed his mother for the death of his sister, whom he never knew.

"I'm not sleeping with goddamned Mary Baker Eddy," he announced one day as he shoved Mom's Bible and *Science and Health with Key to the Scriptures* off the bedside table. He marched from the master bedroom to his wood-paneled office in the back of the property, where he installed an old roll-away cot, only returning to the master bedroom twice a week for a clean shirt.

He'd work long past our bedtime in that office. It reeked of smoke and spilled whiskey. I knew because I had sometimes snuck inside when Dad wasn't around, even though it was forbidden. I'd take one step over the threshold and marvel at the things in there: the painting of the signing of The Declaration of Independence; an old French phone from the 1930s; a hand-cranked adding machine; and about a hundred dusty books in various piles. If Mom knew I was there, it would have been off with my head. Looking back, it was after his retreat to this smoky den when things began to get much worse.

One Saturday morning in 1962, Dad hollered from the living room, "You girls get in here. We have a visitor today and he's going to get to the bottom of things around here." Dad's tone made me feel like I had done something wrong, as he called out for my brothers and clapped his hands. "Move it, move it, move it!" Still in my nightgown, I wiped bits of cinnamon toast from my lips and helped KK untangle herself from the blankets in front of the TV.

Our neighbor, Dr. Craycroft, came through the doorway. He was the kindly father of my brother Don's best friend.

What was he doing here? Walt shot Don a look, who responded with a don't-ask-me shrug. I looked back at KK, a small flannel island standing in front of the fireplace, holding her teddy bear, Lully. We had never seen a real doctor before, let alone had one walk into our living room. Mom was a Christian Scientist, for goodness sake. Did she know about this?

Mom had left early for her volunteer job singing at Kelly Park, like she often did on Saturday mornings. I thought about the last concert of hers I attended. It was fun to run under the shade of the trees and hear her soprano voice amplified for all to hear. When the applause came, it made me feel tingly inside, like I was the special one.

I wish I had gone with her this time. By letting this doctor walk across our carpet, I suddenly felt I had somehow betrayed Mom, but Dad's commands gave me no time to think.

Dad was animated, gesticulating with a sweep of his arm for the doctor to enter the living room, as he barked orders to us. "C'mon get in a straight line. When it's your turn, step forward and tell the doc your age." Dr. Craycroft set down his weathered bag on the seat of Mom's Mozart chair. Was it my imagination or did the carved heads on the armrests seem alarmed?

"I'd like your names, too, if you don't mind," Dr. Craycroft said softly, turning to face us. What was he going to do? Would he give us shots? Would he make us take off our clothes? I folded my arms in front of my chest and wondered what Dad had told him. Did Dr. Craycroft know Mom didn't believe in doctors?

Dr. Craycroft asked each of us a few questions, looked into our mouths and ears. Then he placed a cold metal disk on our chest, like the one Dr. Kildare had on TV. He held it on my skin and asked me to breathe. I wondered why, but didn't ask. We never asked questions when Dad was around. If he said to do something, I did.

At one point, Dr. Craycroft asked if I ever stayed home from school because I wasn't feeling well. I shook my head and refused to mention the stomachaches I had all the time now. They kept me awake at night and at home when I should have been at school. The pain was searing, and I'd clutch my belly for hours as I lay in bed, but I only mentioned them to Mom because talking about them gave them power. Besides, Mom said they weren't real, and I liked staying home with her. She missed me when I was at school.

Dr. Craycroft didn't ask me to get undressed, or poke me with needles or take my temperature, unlike the school nurse last year, who'd examined me when I arrived at school with red dots on my forehead. Dr. Craycroft's touch was gentle, and I enjoyed his attention. But all I could think about was what would happen if Mom came home and saw this? What would she do?

While Don was telling the doctor about missing school because of the measles, Dad got restless. He looked at the clock and turned to Dr. Craycroft. "Are we finished here? I'd like to pick your brain about something important. It's that polio vaccine." I sucked in my breath, remembering friends at school talking about it.

Walt's eyes moved from Dad to Dr. Craycroft, like he was at a tennis match, but I just wanted to cover my ears. Mom had told me all that polio nonsense was just "error" talking. We all knew discussing it gave it power.

Dr. Craycroft pivoted his head toward Dad. "These kids haven't been vaccinated?"

"Nope." Dad leaned his long body against the wall, and tapped a cigarette out of the pack. "As I explained on the phone, my wife. . ."

Dr. Craycroft interrupted. "The government has been encouraging it since when, 1955?" Dad didn't respond, so the doctor tried another tack, softer this time. "How 'bout the usual childhood vaccines? Certainly you. . ."

"Nope." Dad was shaking his head as if the doctor's questions were tedious.

"You mean to tell me these kids aren't protected against smallpox, pertussis, not even tetanus? These are very healthy kids, I'll admit, but all it takes is on wrong step on a rusty nail, and their lives change forever." Dr. Craycroft's voice sounded sharp, like nails were hiding in the carpet, and I stepped back.

Dad shrugged. "It's what the wife wants, and I think she has something there, although the God part is a load of horseshit." Dr. Craycroft closed his eyes. Dad took a long drag on his cigarette and blew a snake of smoke in our direction. I inhaled. Why was Dad being so rude? He was the one who had asked the doctor to come here, to do him a favor. I realized what was going on. It was a trick that Dad was playing, but he wasn't finished.

"Admit it, Doc. These kids are healthy and now you're mad because I popped your bubble by admitting they've never had a vaccine." Dad smiled as he sat on the arm of the couch and leaned toward the doctor, as if examining him. "It's not like we're living in some swamp. They need to get tough to make it in this life."

Dr. Craycroft made a noise in his throat that sounded very like the start of a laugh, and Dad pointed a finger at him. "This rush to vaccinate for every little thing feels like Big Brother, just like Mr. Orwell predicted. You ever read *1984*?" Dad smiled like he had all the answers.

Dr. Craycroft poked his tongue into his cheek. He suddenly seemed so old. "Mr. Erickson, I'm not here to discuss literature. I'm here at your request to look at your children." He looked over at us then, his mouth opening to say something, and then closing. I imagined he was about to yell at Dad. I know I would have.

He turned toward Don and put a hand on his shoulder,

letting it linger there, and I took it as a signal that his exam was over. I wondered what it would be like to have a father touch you so casually. Don was looking down at the carpet, hands in his pockets. I knew he was wondering what the doc say would when he got home. Would he tell his son what had happened here?

The doctor gathered up his medical tools and slipped them into his bag. "I know you've got strong opinions on the subject," he said, "as does your wife. But you're the one who asked me here, and you're the one who asked about the polio vaccine, so I assume you want my advice." He snapped his bag shut.

"What I want, good doctor, is the goddamned truth." Dad leaned over and crushed his cigarette in the ashtray. He might as well have called Dr. Craycroft a liar.

I wanted to run to my room. I looked at Don, who stood in line, his gaze distant, cheeks blossoming red. KK looked up from the floor where she was hugging her knees, listening. I wanted to take her from this room.

Dr. Craycroft moved toward Dad. "Sir, I urge you to take your family to the County Public Health Clinic as soon as possible. There's been talk of Sunday clinics as a convenience for families. That's how important this is." He let the weight of that fall on all of us. Then he walked to the door, with Don at his heels, like a puppy.

***

That evening our grandparents came over for dinner. I loved it when they visited because sometimes Grandpa Louie'd tell old stories. My favorite was the one about the beautiful Blackfoot Indian he dated before he met Grandma and how her parents hated him because he was white.

I had just begun telling him about a history project at school when Dad lifted his fork to his mouth, then said casually, "You're all getting polio shots next week." Four conversations stopped, the words swallowed and forgotten.

Mom looked over at Dad, her face like thunder. It must have seemed like this decision came out of nowhere. She didn't know about Dr. Craycroft's visit, and to make matters worse, keeping it a secret made me nervous. It felt wrong knowing something she didn't. I could see the muscles in her jaw working hard to suppress her response.

"Well, it's about time, Mack," Grandpa Louie said, like he had been waiting for Dad to come to his senses. "Good to know you haven't forgotten about little Louise."

I knew who Louise was, Dad's sister who had died as a baby. I heard myself ask, "Louise?"

Louie spoke slowly. "She was our first-born, ya know. Just a little thing. Back in 1916, when she was almost a year old, she was having difficulty breathing. Your grandma wouldn't let me go get the doctor. Said she'd leave if I did. She prayed everywhere she went: standing at the kitchen sink, sitting in her rocker, in the back yard beneath the sheepberry tree. Everywhere I turned there she was, mouthing words." I looked up at Grandpa Louie, his face giving way to the memory.

"But Louise just got sicker. Then the neighbors got wind of your grandma refusing medical help. There was a rumor she was a witch, and they came to the house with pitchforks one day, meaning to do her harm. That's when a doctor appeared out of nowhere, on horseback. The neighbors parted as he walked up the steps to the porch. He took one look at our little Louise and said she had the polio and there was nothing we could do about it. She was too far gone."

My mind whirled with the word polio, as if it were a hurricane coming to suck us all up into its power.

Grandpa Louie's voice creaked with the weight of the memory. "On his way out, the doctor shooed away the neighbors, telling them to mind their own business, that no medicine in the world could heal that child."

I looked over at Mom, her facial muscles straining as the story wore on. She had too much respect for her father-in-law to contradict his story.

"What happened next?" I asked, unable to see his blue eyes through his foggy glasses.

"Louise died in my arms that afternoon." His sentenced silenced everything except the uneven staccato of my breath. Even Dad was quiet, his face like granite. I linked my arm into Grandpa Louie's, and leaned against his body. Mom reached over and put a hand on his, a kindness that seemed practiced, like she had heard the story a million times before. Why hadn't she ever told me?

Dad pushed his chair back, the scrape of wood jerking our faces up. "Who's up for some ripe watermelon?"

By the time Mom came in to kiss me goodnight, I was bursting with questions I didn't dare ask.

"Don't worry about this polio business, honey. Just do what your father tells you to do. Whether or not you stand in line for a shot doesn't matter, because you know a bit of liquid in a needle simply has no power, don't you?" I nodded, pretending I did. All I felt now was overpowering confusion. She smiled, pulling the comforter under my chin.

The following Sunday, as Mom was dressing for church, Dad marched us out to the car. It felt weird to be in shorts instead of a petticoat and dress. Don claimed shotgun as he ran to front seat. He seemed more energetic now that Dad was following Dr. Craycroft's advice. As I climbed into the back seat, moving over to make room for KK and Walt, my stomach began to cramp. What would the shot be like? Would it burn like my friends said it would? Maybe if I prayed hard enough, I wouldn't feel a thing.

I turned around and looked out the back window of the Impala. Mom stood in the middle of the driveway in her red silk robe that she had thrown on over her girdle and stockings, her arms folded across her chest. Had she thought Dad wouldn't follow through?

As we pulled away, she didn't wave. She didn't even look at me. Her eyes were closed, as if denying she was a witness to our departure. I wanted to jump from the moving car and run to her. I wanted to bury my face in the folds of her robe, like a bee to a flower.

"Ignore your mother," Dad commanded. I spun around, his eyes in the rearview mirror pinning me to my seat.

After that, I tried hard to be the perfect daughter. Although I felt guilty for not telling her about Dad's scheme to have Dr. Craycroft give us secret checkups, I had reasoned that if Dad had ever found out I snitched, he would have been angry. And his anger frightened me. I figured it was just easier to suffer Mom's disappointment. Plus, she'd never hit us.

A couple months later Mom had pretty much forgotten about all of it. I was excited when she suddenly suggested that the two of us go Christmas shopping in downtown Saratoga.

The warmth and hum of the industrial heater hit us as Mom and I entered the old Variety Store on Oak Street. I breathed in the heady aroma of new plastic and books, Juicy Fruit and bicycle tires, and realized this was my idea of heaven. As we passed the register, the clerk nodded at Mom.

"Good morning!" Mom's voice made this a party. "How lovely it is in here, especially since it's so wooshly outside." I loved Mom's made-up words. No other mom I knew did that. If there wasn't a real word that described how she felt, she'd just make one up. Still in her lime green coat with the huge plastic buttons, she crossed her arms in front of her chest and made a little shiver, demonstrating the gust that blew us inside.

Just then a boy stepped up to the register and the clerk turned his attention to the sale of a pack of baseball cards. Maybe that's what I'd get Don for Christmas. I knew the only good thing in that packet was the flat rectangle of Bazooka bubblegum, all powdery and sweet. But Don was big on baseball, so I bet he'd like the cards best.

I pulled Mom toward the toys, smiling to myself. I knew this place like a second home, and the Christmas display with tree lights and decorations, Santas and snowmen made it even better. During any other season I'd walk down the aisles to see if things were in their places, their spots on the shelves so familiar. But today, only one spot beckoned me. By the big front window, was a place filled with wonder: a troll with orange hair, a Breyer model horse too wild to be tamed, and a skintight satin Barbie outfit with shiny black heels. I wanted them all.

I was supposed to be looking for presents for the family, and I felt a little guilty as I pulled Mom over to the toy section, hoping she'd notice the things I loved. We were almost there when I noticed a big poster on the wall. The image stopped me cold. "Who is that?"

Mom looked up at it, tilting her head. "That was our dear president, honey. President Kennedy. You know that."

"No. Who is that little girl he's with? It's not his daughter, Caroline." I had seen a lot of pictures of Caroline on TV. Mom looked at the poster again as if she hadn't noticed the child standing beside the president.

"Oh my, isn't her dress pretty?" Mom squeezed my hand, and I nodded. She reached in her pocketbook and fished for a tissue. It had only been a month since President Kennedy had been shot, and the news was still like a hot coal in her chest. Mom loved him so. We all did, but it was because of her.

I remembered sitting in Mom's lap a few years earlier, watching President Kennedy speak on TV. It was a special talk he was giving. There were important people there, like Mom's favorite opera singer, Marian Anderson, who sang "The Star Spangled Banner," and Robert Frost, who read a poem. Mom sat transfixed as I wiggled in her lap. But when President Kennedy said, ". . . Ask not what your country can do for you, but what you can do for your country," I sat bolt upright at the power of his words. He was like God.

I looked up at the poster again. President Kennedy was sitting in a black leather chair wrapping his arms around the little girl standing next to him, as if she were so light she might float away into the air. Her dress was a rich red, like Mom's lipstick, the only splash of color in the picture except for his blue tie. The frills of her skirt fanned out across the president's knees. In his embrace, she looked like hope in a party dress, the little tiara on her head twinkling.

". . . and that's the Oval Office, the president's special room in the White House. The public isn't usually allowed in there, so I'd say she was a very lucky little girl." Mom winked at me. What had this pretty girl done that made her so important? I marveled at the possibilities and yearned to be special like her. I wanted the president of the United States to wrap his arms around me, too.

The little girl stood there absolutely perfect, except for her legs. "What's are those things?" I said softly, not wanting to destroy the magic of the picture.

"What things, honey?" I looked up at Mom. Didn't she see them? There were metal bands around the child's thin calves, hospital white resting against her flesh. Didn't they

34

pinch her skin? As I looked more closely, I saw that each band had two metal rods connected to a smaller band, farther down at the ankle, the icy shock of them nearly camouflaged by her frilly white socks. I pulled my hand from Mom's and pointed up at the poster, determined to make her notice what I saw.

"Oh, those? Well that's the result of wrong thinking." Mom sounded disapproving, and shook her head sadly, in a some-people-never-learn kind of way. "They call them braces." This last part was matter-of-factly stated, like the last sentence in a book. But I was just getting started.

"Can she walk?" I was now standing as close as I could to the poster without going behind the counter.

The cashier behind the register was listening. He leaned his long body in our direction, his hand resting on a white collection can, labeled "March of Dimes." He opened his mouth to speak, but Mom glared at him, her lips pushing forward to warn him away from responding. She bent over and whispered, her stiff bubble hairdo hovering, her hot breath at my ear. "Of course she can, honey. She's God's perfect child."

I turned my head to look at Mom. Her red lips were pressed together, thin and unflattering. Not another syllable escaped her mouth. She stood up, her chin high, and looked straight at the cashier as if he were adding to her difficulties. Where was the happy Mom I had walked in with? Taking my hand, she pulled me toward the door. I tripped in the sudden movement, and embarrassed, looked back over my shoulder at the clerk. His brow wrinkled as he caught my gaze. I quickly looked away and covered my eyes as we walked out into the harsh winter light.

CHAPTER THREE

I ached to understand. Mom's explanations of her religious beliefs made no sense, but I was caught in her web. I wanted to believe. My brothers came up with a million reasons not to go to church, so by the time I was nine years old, they were off the hook and only KK and I were expected to go. Each Sunday Dad would position my brothers, then thirteen and fifteen, on the back patio at 9:30 a.m. He'd hand them each a beer, and they'd lean back and wait. We would swish past their laughter in crinoline and patent leather shoes, and climb into the car for Sunday school.

We never spoke of it, but I felt ashamed for Mom. By then I knew not all men treated their wives like Dad treated Mom. I had become a great observer of my friends' dads, and knew my dad was different. I'd listened to them talk and they'd invite me into their conversations in a you're-part-of-our-family kind of way that made my chest hurt. In particular, my best friend Julie's dad would go out if his way to include me, joking and encouraging laughter. I love the attention, but wanted it from my own father.

Each time I'd return home from a friend's house I vowed to try harder. After all, Dad wasn't that bad. He'd spend almost every night after dinner lecturing us. He'd scrape his chair back, walk over to the chalkboard on the kitchen door, and cover it in figures and drawings, explaining some scientific principle. I usually had no idea what he was talking about, but I sat upright, eyes wide open, pretending to be his star student.

One day I stood in the kitchen facing Dad's back as he thrust his arms under the faucet and scrubbed his forearms. "You want me to go where?" His face was red from the sun, his eyes adjusting to the light in the kitchen. Rivulets of soil streamed down Dad's arms.

"A father–daughter picnic," I said, still hopeful. He was busy scrubbing his arms, the electric green Palmolive dish soap foaming up to his elbows.

"Why only fathers?" Dad asked.

My face flushed. Since I had only recently joined Campfire, I didn't know the answer. I knew lots of other stuff like Campfire was the first nonsectarian and multicultural organization for girls in America, something very important to Mom. It also had a Native American theme. We earned beads, not badges. We sold candy, not cookies. And now we were about to celebrate fathers by hosting a father–daughter picnic.

Dad's foot was tapping, waiting for a response. Apparently he hadn't heard about the proposed National Father's Day, so I rushed to tell him about it.

"Our Campfire leader said the picnic is an annual tradition. It celebrates dads! They've been doing it for years, in fact long before the idea of making a holiday for dads, like there is for moms."

"Mother's Day is not a holiday, it's just a day carved out for florists and greeting card companies to make money." Dad scrubbed his skin with his fingernails.

"But the money will go to a good cause." I moved so I could see his face. Maybe I could convince him with my smile.

"Ah. So that's it. What will this put me back?" He turned and vigorously wiped a dishtowel over his arms.

"Each Campfire girl makes a special lunch to share with her dad, and puts it in decorated box so it doesn't look like anyone else's. Then while the dads hide their eyes, we put our boxes on the table and the fun begins."

Dad rolled his eyes, but I plowed ahead. "Each dad bids on the one that his daughter made, but sometimes dads goof up or pretend to, and start bidding on someone else's lunch. Last year Molly's dad offered ten dollars for another girl's lunch, and the two dads were getting louder and louder pretending to argue while they were bidding. Molly said everybody was cracking up."

"Sounds like a lot of hooey just to make a few bucks. Why not just tell the truth—that the troop's a little short, and needs a handout?" I didn't like how he made it sound like we were thieves, but I was undeterred.

"It's gonna be fun, you'll see. It's at Molly's house, and they just got a pool. There's a diving board!" I remembered a cannonball jump Dad did last summer and how we squealed with the splash as it fell on us as we lay at the rim sunning ourselves.

Dad hooked the towel around the fridge handle, one eyebrow raised.

Mom slipped into the kitchen, as if on cue. "Oh, that sound like fun, now doesn't it?" She addressed herself to the fading yellow wallpaper, but something in her words punched Dad in the gut. My eyes bounced back and forth from Dad to Mom to Dad as their eyes yelled at each other.

Mom's chin was tight as she spoke. "Mack, it's just a sweet little gathering, and a lot of effort will be going into it. All of the fathers are going."

"Not this one." Dad's lips were pursed as if he were about to spit.

"Mack, this is important." Mom put a manicured hand on her hip.

"To whom? Certainly not to me, and I bet I'm not alone. That Campfire Girl outfit should ask dads how we'd like to spend our day. I'm certain it wouldn't include being on the receiving end of this goddamned grief."

Mom's words were moored in her throat as the sound of Dad's boots marched out the back door, an audible blast of air escaping between his lips. At the slam of the screen door, I realized I hadn't been breathing. I looked over at Mom, my eyes pleading with her: Did I do something wrong? Would I be the only girl at the picnic without a father? Who would bid on *my* lunch box? I imagined the looks on the fathers' faces, and their daughters' too, as they clung to their fathers with unspoken relief. I felt the heat rise on my face, a confusion of embarrassment and anger.

If they asked, I'd say that Dad had wanted to come to the picnic, but something important had come up at work and he needed to care of it. Maybe they'd even believe me. After all, he'd recently quit his boring job at the bank to begin his land development corporation. Following his dream of being his own boss was good for all of us all, wasn't it? It might even make him happy.

The fantasy folded in on itself as the weight of Dad's words fell onto my shoulders. Just a year ago Dad had discovered the beauty of the Sierras, surrounded by the grit and glory of the California gold rush, a three-hour drive from our home. Nothing had been the same after that. In fact, each day the change stole into our lives taking with it something of value.

Dad's dream was like a fever. In his bones he knew Pine Grove was a great place to live, with its cheap land and stunning views, where a person could walk all day and not see another soul, and yet drive two hours down the road and attend the symphony in Sacramento. It was the best of both worlds. Who wouldn't love it? He bought up land and began building homes for others who shared his dream of solitude. After that he lived each day as if failure were chasing him. Even his body leaned into the battle, preparing to plow through superfluous events, like my picnic.

Perhaps I should have known better than to invite him, but when Dad walked out the door, something inside of me slammed shut. I called Grandpa Louie, who quickly agreed to take me to the picnic. "I'd be honored to be your guest. What's for lunch?" His voice sounded light but I could tell worry stood at the edge of it. I knew he wouldn't pry and I suddenly felt lucky he'd be the one accompanying me.

At the Father Daughter picnic, my grandfather never mentioned Dad. He joked with all the other men and taught my friends how count to ten in Swedish. He bid on my lunch and told me my turkey sandwich was the best lunch in the whole world. He even danced to Ray Charles singing "Hit the Road Jack," his long legs stepping to the beat, his eyes fixed on the far wall. Was he wondering why Dad wasn't here? Grandpa Louie was the best stand-in father I could have hoped for, and I loved him for making me smile. But when everyone changed into bathing suits, the day fell to pieces.

I stepped out of the changing room in my new red bathing suit, and found Grandpa Louie all alone, lying fully clothed on the chaise lounge in the shade of the patio. He hadn't even kicked off his loafers. I grabbed a pool chair and moved it next to him, the fabric of the webbing cutting into the back of my thighs.

We sat motionless, like wounded birds. His pale flesh stood out in sharp contrast to the fathers with their taut, tanned limbs moving through the water like seals. They dunked their daughters and yelled "Marco! Polo!" We were invisible.

I was tired of watching. "Want some more lemonade?"

"Naw, I got plenty here. You go get in that pool. You don't need to sit with me just because I can't swim. You can go have fun with the other kids." For a moment I saw myself in my new bathing suit doing a surprise cannonball leap into the pool. I could feel the water close in over me, silencing my thoughts. What was the real reason Dad hadn't come today? Was it something I had done?

"That's okay, I like being here with you. Besides, my stomach kind of hurts." I sat back in my pool chair and turned my face away.

When I entered Mom's bedroom after the picnic, she was lying across her bed reading the newspaper.

"How was it, honey?" She pushed the newspaper aside and propped herself up onto an elbow. I told her everything.

"Oh honey, I think you just need to butter your dad up a bit. Ask about things he's interested in." She reached over and turned the page of the article she was reading. It sounded like the crackle of fire. I thought about what we had in common. I made a mental list of topics he'd know a lot about:

1. The German national anthem
2. Hemmingway and Poe
3. How submarines work
4. How to load a handgun
5. What's the proper technique for sharpening the meat cleaver?
6. How does sulfur dry apricots?

Would I really have to learn the German national anthem to get my father to go to a picnic? It sounded like a trick an older girl would play on a boy she likes, cooing and pretending to like his baseball card collection so he would ask her out on a date. You'd have to drag me through a scorching desert wasteland with no water for a week before I'd ever do that.

I thought back to earlier in the day, being the only girl without her father. The heat rose on my face, stemming from the embarrassment and anger at being singled out, and suddenly I knew Mom was right, I had to go find him. The screen door hissed and slapped closed behind me as I stepped out into the sunshine.

I could barely make Dad out, framed by a brilliance of leaves, sitting on the edge of a cot in the orchard, beneath the shade of an avocado tree. Staring out of the shadows, his gaze was weightless, the sun resting its heat on the tips of his boots that stood like sentries to his private shelter. I rubbed my sweaty palms on my shorts. Was I nuts for heading out there? I had something to ask him, but couldn't it wait? I stood back and watched, and tried to remember the list I had just made.

"Dad, I'd like to learn about—" Oh crap. What was on that list? I spotted the box of gardening tools at Dad's feet. "What are those for?" Did I seem interested?

Sitting a few feet above Dad in the tree, a sparrow called out from her nest. He glanced up, then took a drag on his Viceroy, exhaling a long snake of cigarette smoke.

"Grafting. They're the tools that were used at the Tree Circus in Santa Cruz. Remember when we saw them?" He glanced back at me. Was he smiling? "Do you want to learn how to graft fruit trees?"

My thoughts swarmed like bees. Had Dad just asked me what I wanted? I didn't care what it was. Anything. "Yes!" I spread my fingers against my chest, nodding like a bobble-head. No way was I going to tell him the truth: that I was buttering him up so he'd like me.

Memories of visiting that old Tree Circus haunted me. Some seventy trees were contorted into some manner of madness, forced to grow at disturbing angles and curves. I hadn't forgotten that the trees had been harmed in order to do this.

Against my better judgement, I bent down and peered at the grafting tools so Dad wouldn't see my frozen smile, but he was already heading toward the peach trees. "Follow me. Best way to get good at anything is watch a master, then try it yourself. " He made a slight detour to gather the chainsaw from the garage. A crow cackled on the fence. It sounded like laughter.

I clapped my hands over my ears at the sound of the chainsaw.

Dad shouted over the din. "Make a cut into the mother tree, like this." Lifting the chainsaw, he sliced off the strong arms of the biggest peach tree in our orchard. In less than five minutes, she'd been reduced to a trunk with two large amputated stubs jutting upward, like a child begging to be held. What had he done?

Dropping to his knees, Dad gripped a stub on the trunk, where a limb used to be, and stabbed it with a grafting knife, right at the bark line. When he could force it no further by hand, he tapped the blade into the wood with a grafting hammer. He pried it out and jammed it into her again. He said he was making a hole for a new branch to fit in.

I wanted to stroke her bark and apologize. I wanted to lay my palm on her cuts. I wanted to run. Stepping back, I squeezed my wet eyes closed, imagining what she would have looked like in another month: dozens of yellow globes, summer's exquisite perfume lifting into the air.

"What's wrong with you?" Dad scraped the bits of wood out from the V-shaped hole he had been carving in the amputated stub. "Get over here and look. This is where the baby branch will be inserted." He pushed the back of my head in close. "See that spring green layer, right beneath the bark? That's where germination takes place."

"Oh!" The surprise of this was like the promise of magic. The green encircled the branch stub like a slender jade bracelet. A secret code just for me. Had Dad done a good thing? The back of my throat squeezed shut. No. How dare we hack off her arms, peek into her interior, expose her secret?

"Now listen up. The whole point of grafting is to have one tree support more than one type of fruit. Today you're going to graft apricot branches onto the peach tree." Dad reached into a bucket and handed me a slender apricot branch. There were three buds on it, a dark red film over each, splitting open to a soft pink, the color of my ballet shoes. He'd cut it from another tree earlier, and now it was in my hands.

Dad continued describing the process. I would now carve the bark off the cut end of my baby apricot branch and expose the green layer underneath. Then I'd stick it into the wedge he'd made in the mother peach trunk. The peach tree would now feed the apricot branch.

"Make sure the branch will fit in nice and snug. The green cambium layers have to touch, so be careful. It's easy to damage it." My hand shook. This wasn't my idea, or was it? Why wasn't he going to demonstrate exactly what to do?

"What happens if I get it wrong?"

"Just don't injure the branch by making the cut too sharp, that's all. It needs to be a wedge, or it'll die." He pinched the bridge of his nose and closed his eyes.

What if I mess up? I dropped the knife. "Dad, I can't do it."

His hand thwacked down hard on the sawed-off trunk. "You sure as hell can." His face sparkled with sweat.

My throat tightened further. "I'll hurt it!" There. I'd finally said it.

"Jesus H. Christ." He cuffed the knife from the ground and wiped it on his knees, stabbing it in the air as he spoke. "Trees don't feel anything."

He was lying. If they didn't feel pain, then why had he said last weekend, "How would you like it if somebody ripped off your arm?" when I accidentally broke a stem while weeding some flowers? When I turned to face him, he was yelling at me.

"You're the one who wanted to learn to graft." He held out the knife to me. "And I'm telling you that the little branch you're holding isn't going to start screaming like a girl."

Something inside me shifted. It was like watching myself through a wall of glass. I saw my arm slowly reach out and take the knife out of his hand. I saw the buds on my apricot branch, their soft heads cradled against my left arm. I saw my head pivot and look him straight in the face. Then I heard myself say, "I can't do it. I never even wanted to learn to graft." I lifted my chin and held his gaze.

Dad turned, staring out at the orchard. It was so quiet in that moment, just the soft spring breath trembling leaves on the fruit trees.

Oh God, I blew it. What would he do? Could I take it back? "Dad?" I placed my slender apricot branch on the stump, along with the knife. "I could help you by painting the graft with the tree tar. I could do that. I just don't want to harm the little branch."

He turned, shaking his head, one fist clenching and unclenching. "We're done here."

I bolted to the front of the property, to the huge pine tree that heralded the beginning of our driveway. This had been my safe place whenever I needed to be not found. Anxious, I moved beneath the tree in a sort of dance, trying to forget what I had just done. I imagined this steady pine with its huge arms leaning toward me, hearing my thoughts, comforting me. I could have made things better with Dad. I could have followed his orders, gripped the knife, and sliced the branch. Why hadn't I done it?

CHAPTER FOUR

A few weeks later I was standing in the hallway outside my parents' bedroom. Mom didn't see me peeking around the open door as she moved about her room preparing to go out. I wasn't sure where she was going that evening, but she was dressing for something special, like the opera. She turned to check her reflection in the big maple vanity mirror, her girdle tight, the skin above it glistening with freedom.

Moments before, she had reached into her closet, gathered up the hem of her green satin dress, disappeared inside the skirt of it, lifted her arms into the air and slipped it over her shoulders. The green continued its journey downward, framing the curves of her breasts and waist and exposing her décolletage perfectly, before shooting out at her hips, the crinoline petticoat making a soft "shush" sound as she moved.

Mom leaned toward the mirror and removed the crystal lid of her perfume bottle, dabbing the pink enamel tip of it down her neck, the scent of Chanel No. 5 whispering secrets of the evening ahead. Two opera tickets and her mother-of-pearl opera glasses were waiting for her like old friends atop the vanity table. She picked them up, placing them tenderly into her evening bag. I wished I had been invited.

Not long ago Dad had announced that he would no longer join her at the opera, given all the work he had to do now that he worked for himself. He flicked a hand into the air as he spoke. "Besides, it's an awfully long way to drive to watch some overblown buffoons prance around on stage pretending to be lovers."

Although Mom's eyebrow arched and there was surprise in her voice, she recovered from Dad's decision quickly, inviting Grandpa Louie or dear friends to accompany her on opera evenings.

I knew there was more to Dad's decision than that because I had overheard my parents discussing the check that arrived each month addressed to Mom. It came in a creamy white envelope with "Bank of New York" on the envelope. I recall Dad's words, too, barely audible in the hallway outside my bedroom, more a hiss than a statement, "I don't want your money. I've work hard for mine. So if you want to waste your inheritance on season tickets to the opera or bleeding heart causes or music lessons for the kids, that's your business."

On opera nights, Dad would often leave shortly after Mom did, on an errand of some kind in town. In the past, whenever that happened, my big sister Margery was given the job to watch us, which always made her cranky. But now that she was off at college, we were left with Dad. And sometimes he'd leave anyway.

I worried about being left alone. I looked over at Mom, getting ready for the evening. "Do you really have to go?" I blurted into the silence. Even as I said it I knew there was no point. She was always getting dressed up and going out, as if she led two lives—one with us, and another far more glamorous and maybe even more important. My stomach clenched at the thought.

"Of course I do, honey." Mom smiled and stepped forward, bending low to kiss my left cheek. Although our cheeks touched, she pushed her lips out dramatically, kissing the air instead—to protect her lipstick. Her gloves dangled graciously from her hands resting briefly on my skin, and I breathed in her elegance.

Mom stole a glimpse at her watch. "Goodness, look at the time!" She grabbed her evening bag off the bed and fled out the door, calling out, "Have fun this evening!"

An hour later, a delivery truck pulled up with a huge container for my father. I was terribly curious, but Dad shooed us out of the way until the thing had been uncrated and the deliveryman had left.

"You kids can come out here now." Dad called us into the living room. He swept his hand lovingly along the sleek grain of the wood. Was this what I thought it was?

Inside the cabinet, a hi-fi stereo with six dials and an automatic turntable gleamed - a 1962 state-of-the-art surprise for Mom. I'd seen it in TV commercials. Would I be allowed to play it?

Dad talked about that stereo all the way through dinner. "Just wait 'til you hear that beauty. It's like having the orchestra right there in the living room!"

I'd never seen so much grinning on his face before. It altered everything.

As dinner came to a close, Dad announced his plan to play Beethoven that evening, and to demonstrate for us the power of the stereo—which garnered a groan from my brother Don.

"Aw, Dad. Do I have to?" Don rolled his eyes.

Dad's face fell, but I could see he wasn't going to make Don stick around. That's when I realized Don slithered out of nearly everything he didn't like.

Don was already standing, feet turned toward the door.

"C'mon Dad, it's our sixth-grade science fair tomorrow, and I've still got stuff to do. I don't have time to waste listening to music by a guy who died a hundred years ago."

I sucked in my breath at his disrespect. I would have dropped everything to be in the room with Dad's grin, but Don didn't seem to notice Dad's happiness. He didn't even have a science project, as far as I knew. He just wanted out, preferring to spend his time in his room with his dirty fingernails—reading mechanics magazines and taking apart old radios to see how they worked. Dad jerked his head toward the door, and let him go.

My brother Walt sat across from me at the table, watching Don's exit, his face darkening, legs twitching to leave. Don had just beat him at his own game, and there was no way Dad would let them both them off the hook. Secretly, I was glad Walt was still at the table. He was fourteen, and always had some smarty-pants response to things that I wouldn't dare say aloud. He was the one who had given KK and me our first cigarette, wrote lyrics that made no sense, and took time to play duets on the piano with KK even though there was an eight-year difference between them.

Now he was busting to retreat to his room to listen to an album by a brand new artist named Bob Dylan. Walt leaned toward me and said, "You gotta hear him man, he's like nothing you've ever heard before." Walt's passion made me smile, and I believed him.

"Bah!" Dad spat out. "What do rock n' rollers know about music? Now, Mr. Beethoven—he was a real musician. You'll see. You three meet me in the living room after you've cleaned up the kitchen."

I looked over at the huge pile of dirty pots and plates. Walt would make some important excuse to retreat elsewhere for fifteen minutes. Cleanup was left to KK and me. I thought of my book report that was due the next day—and I still had all those spelling words to memorize. I'd have to stay up late to finish everything. How long would this demonstration take?

―――――――――――――

KK, Walt and I walked into the living room. Dad turned, and in a grand gesture, swept one hand, palm up, toward the stereo. "Just look at this beauty. Your mother's going to love it." I knew she would. I could just imagine the soulful voices of Marian Anderson and Leontyne Price, warming the room like sunlight.

We gathered, staring at the glistening knobs as Dad fiddled with this one, then that one, but the best part was that automatic arm. I couldn't believe my eyes when Dad pressed the lever. It floated over and landed softly onto the record, like magic.

"Are the speakers any good?" Walt asked, breaking the spell. "I mean, does the music lose quality if you crank it up?" Dad ignored him, and I plopped on the couch to wait for the music to begin.

"Get off that couch." Dad's words were suddenly raw. "You've got a job to do. The three of you spread out on the floor, in a semicircle shape, like an orchestra—and face me." My eyebrows scrunched together. I wanted the happy dad back, but something had changed him. Was it my fault? I peeked over at Walt, who lifted a shoulder in response to my unasked question.

We sat on the floor exactly as Dad told us to. "Now. We all know you two are musicians," Dad began, poking a finger in the air at little KK, and then at Walt. It was true. The two of them practiced on our great-grandmother's big black piano for hours every day, not because they were told to, but because they loved to. How could I ever compete with them?

But I was also a musician, wasn't I? Why else would Mom ask me to sing with her around the grand piano in the evenings? Wasn't I the one who always looked for a way to harmonize with a melody? It wasn't the piano or a violin, but I could pick out perfect harmonies, no matter what song was playing.

Dad's voice boomed as his lecture continued. "Now, there's a message just waiting to be discovered in every piece of music, but you can't really understand the message, unless you pay close attention. It's like a secret language that you need to decipher." Walt rolled his eyes and looked over at me, shaking his head. Dad didn't seem to notice.

"You all know Beethoven's Ninth Symphony. But what we're going to hear is the one that came right before it, written in the summer of 1812 while our man Beethoven was trying to find a cure for his progressive hearing loss. You'd think that he'd give up, or that his music would have been gloomy. But no! He was so confident about his work, he produced this gem."

Walt whispered, "He may have been a genius, but he was also an arrogant asshole." My eyes went wide at the forbidden swear word, but I liked the power it had. I whispered it under my breath to see what it felt like. My skin tingled.

Dad jerked his head at us. "Stop muttering. This is important. No matter what you do in life, you have to have confidence, and Beethoven had it in spades. Did you know that once, when he was accosted by a nasty critic after a performance, instead of boo-hooing about it, he responded, 'What I shit is better than anything you could ever think up.' Now that's confidence for you. That's Mr. Beethoven."

Dad turned his back to us and lifted the top of the cabinet, as he slipped the record out of its sleeve and placed it on the turntable. "So tonight we'll play the Eighth Symphony, and I will be the conductor. I'll tell you when to come in, so keep a sharp eye out for me."

"When to come in?" I asked.

"You heard me. You will play when I tell you to, and not a moment before. Listen and watch." He closed his eyes, and lifted a pencil, which appeared out of nowhere. Walt gawked at me as we both realized this was Dad's baton.

The music burst forth from the speakers and we jumped. Dad's arm shot out and he pointed at Walt, whose smirk evaporated in the blast of sound. Walt stared wild-eyed as Dad's head jerked to the pounding of the thunderous kettle drums, strands of his hair tossed into the air.

Then all at once the music slowed and filled with mystery, which drew me into Dad's imagining as I saw myself dancing alone on a stage, like Clara in The Nutcracker, leaping and spinning late into Christmas Eve. Dad looked at me, eyebrows lifted, as if he were telling a secret, and put one finger from his free hand to his lips as the music diminished.

I looked over at KK who was curled up on the carpet. Would Dad get mad? To cover for her, I moved my imaginary bow slowly across my imaginary strings, as if I really could soften the sound. The violins vibrated from the speakers, building suspense, and Dad shook his free hand as if shaking off water.

Then the music darkened, as a heartbreak of chords told of tragedy, sadness melted through my body. I couldn't help but watch Walt in the percussion section, who was now on his knees, fluidly moving from kettle drums to cymbals as if he had been doing this every night of his life. His face was scrunched up, eyebrows one long line, his whole body pulsing to the beat.

My heart clenched. The music shifted. It was as if I was striding up a grassy hill returning home after a long absence, and once there, looked down at the valley below, my homeland, only to see devastation scarring the land. French horns brought to mind past battles and memories of loss. But embedded in the sound of the woodwinds and strings was defiance and resilience, as the music climbed to a tortuous intensity.

Beautiful and tragic. Slow and fast. Soft and loud. Each contrast twisted together into one. I thought of stolen visions I spied as I walked home from school: Dad's stoic reflection in the garden, his hand reaching up into the branches to pick fruit. My thoughts moved to his sandpaper words, his cutting refusal to attend anything I was involved in. Somehow all of it was right here in the music.

My father wasn't this thing or that—he was all of it. The nurturer. The neglectful. The frightening. The brilliant. The longing for him to love me wove a pattern of exquisite beauty with the harmony of the music, and it was this that kept me rooted to the carpet at his feet.

Dad thrust out his arm, palm down, moving as if stirring a huge pot of notes, swirling and blending them together. I was so mesmerized by his hand movement that when Dad next stabbed his baton in the air above me, I scrambled to understand what he wanted me to do.

I realized that Dad didn't intend for me to be one single musician, playing one specific instrument. When he pointed, I had to play whatever came next, anything from oboe to kettle-drums. And when I responded to his cue, his eyes would close briefly and relax. His mind, just steps ahead, preparing for what was yet to come.

Dad's eyes flew open moments later, wide and expectant, like a madman, reminding me of a photo I had recently seen of Einstein, hair sticking out at angles. In that instant I thought of my best friend Julie's perfect father with his grey suit and combed hair, cracking jokes and asking how Julie's day was. Right now he'd be huddled over the kitchen table helping her with her homework. What was it like to have a father like that? Would her dad ever turn into Beethoven in the evening?

CHAPTER FIVE

After that night, things seemed to be looking up at home. Dad had quit his job at the bank, and he'd even started to whistle. He wasn't home as often, but when he was, he'd talk about the importance of working for himself and having a good work ethic. But most of all, he'd speak of his big plans to develop land in the Sierras, making home sites for people just like us who wanted a quiet life, away from the city.

Sometimes that plan scared my mother. She would clear her throat or pucker her lips when he'd suggest moving from our home in the Bay Area to the Sierra Nevada Mountains, and sometimes he'd even say the thing that frightened her the most: that there'd be no symphony or opera or museums for a hundred miles. But Dad's dream was hypnotic, and eventually we were all caught in his spell. Especially me.

It wasn't long before Dad bought a cattle ranch in the heart of gold rush country in Amador County, and that's when things began to change. Dad's seemingly happier mood made an abrupt turn for the worse. Having already refused to join Mom at the opera, he now stopped joining us on family outings of any kind, preferring to spend all of his time on his plans for the Sierras.

But according to Mom's stash of photographs, we had the best of both worlds, moving seamlessly between our two homes, a picture perfect family smiling into the camera. In the Bay Area we attended school, visited museums and the opera, spent long weekends at the wharf, sipping chowder and watching hippies dance in the street. We wore patent leather shoes and itchy white gloves and Mom charmed the waiters with her décolletage.

At the ranch, nobody cared a damn about any of that— especially my father, who said he could finally breathe. He paraded around in dirty jeans and boots like he just crawled out of a goldmine, and I loved him for it. With the Ponderosa pines to our backs, we'd look at the purple rim of the Sierra Nevada Mountains and listen to the whinnies of the horses. On the surface, a perfect family.

Throughout the school year, we'd live in the Saratoga and spend school vacations and many weekends at the ranch, a three hour drive away. Although the rest of my siblings tolerated the time in the Sierras, I think I was the only one who adored it. In the summer we'd leave home immediately after school let out, and not return until a few days before the new school year started.

I loved the difference each place offered. Home provided ballet and music lessons, the Santa Cruz Boardwalk, San Francisco's museums and my best friend Julie. Our home was set at the base of the lush Santa Cruz Mountains, and the beach was just thirty minutes away.

But in the Sierras I was content with the big sky and quiet. I would wear comfortable, mismatched clothes, and ride horses whenever I wanted. I could get dirty and not take a shower for a week. At times I felt guilty that I loved it so much, especially when I thought of Julie back home, who hated our absence, but in no time after our return for the school year, she'd forgive us and we'd be back to normal.

One summer morning in the Sierras, I was walking back to the ranch house from visiting the horses in the pasture, thinking about the upcoming school year. I didn't want to leave the ranch and start fifth grade. I was beginning to like Dad's idea of moving up here for good. I stepped into the ranch house and stood stock still at the sight of Dad sitting at the dining room table, holding a rifle, and my brother Don leaning in to look at it.

"A man needs to protect and feed his family," Dad was explaining, as he plunged the bore brush into the barrel. My brother Don was all ears. He'd been asking for a rifle for years. "And this rifle needs cleaning." Dad spied me standing there in my shorts and cowboy boots, and motioned me over. "Don't just stand there—time to learn something." I held my breath. Did Mom know about this gun? Was it as off limits as the revolver in Dad's desk at home? I walked slowly in his direction. Hadn't I heard about a guy in the news who shot himself while cleaning his gun?

"Aw Dad, Chuckwagon doesn't need to know this stuff," Don complained looking over at me like this was my idea. I bristled at my nickname. Dad ignored the comment, holding the rifle upright, gripping just below the muzzle and securing the butt between his dirty boots, his right hand pulling the brush out for us to examine. "This rifle needs cleaning, and I'm going to show you both how to do it."

"Yuk," I said, leaning in closer. I rubbed my nose at the sharp stink of it.

"That's debris in the barrel. It affects the course of the bullet, and it could make you miss your target." He looked from the barrel to me, his next words slower, as if they were moving through sludge. "And you never want to miss your target." That's when Dad announced that he had an unusual chore for Don and me.

I hadn't expected this lesson to turn into a chore, but you never knew with Dad. The job he proposed was for Don and me to shoot a tree at thirty yards out with the Winchester. I stood there in my shorts and cowboy boots taking in his every word. I don't know why I was surprised that Dad was so easy around guns. But right now I could almost imagine him in the Wild West, galloping over the hills with the Winchester strapped to his saddle.

My stomach bubbled, excited that Dad thought I was big enough to be a part of this job. But Don wasn't having any of it. He looked down at the ground as we stood in the pasture, rolling his eyes at Dad's instructions.

"That's your target, right there." Dad stabbed a finger in the air at the long trunk of the Ponderosa pine just outside the pasture. "You're trying for the third branch from the bottom."

I squinted at the branch, but it didn't help. Sometimes I had a tough time seeing things at a distance, but last summer I surprised everybody by being good at archery. Maybe I would be good at this too.

"Now when you pull the trigger, you're gonna feel a little surprise kickback on your shoulder. It's just a little push. You'll get over it. Remember, just plant your feet like this, and hold your ground." Dad dug his boot heels into the red earth, then looked over at me, handing me the rifle. I didn't move from my shooting stance. I wanted to be perfect. Dad leaned on the big metal cattle gate and lit a cigarette.

I lifted the rifle and got the third branch in my sites. Dad trusted me and I had to do it right. I took my time and thought back to last August when I became consumed by archery. How the thrill of a bull's eye made my body electric. I blinked and settled my eyes on the Ponderosa.

My breath caught at a flutter of wings settling on the lower branches. No way was I going to shoot at them. I eyed Dad, who was staring at my every move. Would he notice what I was about to do? Moving a fraction to the right, I pulled the trigger at the blue sky between the branches. The force of the kickback made me stumble backwards as two crows flew skyward, cawing their surprise as they flapped to safety. Convinced Dad knew I had missed on purpose, I masked my face with a grimace and clutched my shoulder, the rifle dangling at my knees.

"Jesus, what a lousy shot that was!" Dad guffawed, shaking his head. "Do it again, and this time, do exactly as I told you." Dad blew a blast of cigarette smoke out of his nose, just like a dragon.

I shook my head. "My shoulder hurts," I lied. I looked back at little KK who had been sitting on a high mound of earth behind me, watching. Could she tell I was faking?

Dad spat and moved toward me. "Girls." He cuffed the rifle and handed it to Don. "Let's see what boys can do." I hated Dad at that moment.

Don shrugged, lifting the rifle neatly into place. Just like that, he shot a spray of bark off the third branch. Within three days' time he'd perfected his skill and shot a little bat right out of the evening sky, calling us all over to check it out as it writhed and cried on an old bit of newspaper he'd laid out of the floor of the garage to display his black trophy. I hadn't expected him to do it. It was a harmless baby flying around following its mom. It wasn't even a pest. I added Don to my hate list.

The next morning I was jolted awake by shouting as I lay in the top bunk of the bedroom I shared with KK. Then there came quick boot steps on the wooden floor and the thwack of the screen door. Seconds later, I could hear Dad shouting to Sid, our cowhand, who lived over the tack room by the stables. Sid had a bristle of white hair and was built hard and gnarled like an old scrub oak, and he always made a point of helping me when he could. Out on the trail we'd worked out a routine that we never tired of. He'd trot up alongside me on his horse, reach into his flannel pocket and produce a small bag of tobacco.

"Care for some snuff?" He'd lift an eyebrow and open the bag just a little, shaking the leaves for me to see.

"Eww!" I'd squeal and turn away, and he'd chuckle. I never let on that I actually longed to pinch the crushed leaves and tuck them into my cheek like he did.

"You sure?" He'd cock his head and pull a face. Then he'd cluck to his horse and break into a trot to join Dad, who always led the way, even if Sid was the one who really knew the territory.

More shouts came from the front of the ranch house bringing me back to whatever it was going on outside. Dad's truck engine started up and the tires rolled over gravel. It was early. Had a new horse arrived? I peered down at KK in the bottom bunk, curled under the covers. A fat ray of sunshine fingered the wood floor, dust motes dancing in the spotlight. It was going to be hot today. I sprang off the top bunk and threw on my jeans, t-shirt and boots, and tiptoed out of the room.

Dad's boots raised a low cloud of dust as he slammed the truck door and marched toward the massive spreading oak that stood in the front of the house. Sid was throwing a wire cable over the largest limb of the tree, and fastening it with hooks. What was he doing? I pushed opened the old screen door to get a better look.

"Make yourself useful," Dad barked when he heard the

screen door squeak. "Go get that young heifer we brought up from the Ridge Road pasture."

"D'you mean Rosie?" I asked, the name flying right into the air before I caught myself. Dad didn't approve of naming anything but horses and dogs. I headed for the corral, my boots moving fast.

"Who named her that?" Dad called out, but I pretended I was too far away to hear him. He wouldn't have approved.

Part of Dad's dream of the Sierras was to live the life of a wealthy rancher. Friends used to say it was like he was born too late, that he'd be better suited to living a hundred years ago, all rough and tumble. His favorite TV show was the western, *Bonanza*. Already he had amassed twelve horses and fifty head of cattle, and they just kept coming. He never paid top dollar for them. Never poured over ads in the paper for the perfect specimen. No, he'd found them at livestock auctions or won them in gambling games.

He sold some of his cattle for meat, but mostly he just liked to have them around, moving over the fields, laying about in groups under the spreading oaks. He'd drive along Ridge Road and point out his fortune with a wave of his hand.

Three weeks ago, when Rosie had been moved from the pasture to our ranch, she had seemed lonely, removed from the rest of the herd. Even her moo was sad. Since I was responsible for feeding and watering her, I gave her a name, but up 'til now, I'd kept it to myself. I felt like a dope for spilling the beans.

"She's a heifer, not a cow," Sid said that first day when I was filling her water trough with a battered hose.

"What?" I turned to look at him.

"A female bovine is a heifer until she has a calf," Sid called over his shoulder as he scooped up a bucket of oats. I loved it when he told me facts like this. His teachings poured out of him at every opportunity.

I haltered Rosie and led her out of the corral. She was headstrong, and even though I pulled her along, she was the one in control. I stumbled this way and that as she lumbered off the path to munch grass, Dad watching my every move, shaking his head with that grin on his face.

Dad leaned the Winchester against the base of the oak tree where Sid had just finished securing those cables to the tree. He mumbled something to Sid that I couldn't make out, and Sid looked up, seeming surprised I was leading Rosie. He met me at the big cattle gate.

"You go inside," Sid said softly. I obeyed.

"What are they doing out there?" I asked Mom when I stepped back into the ranch house, a half hour later. She and KK were making cinnamon toast, and they joined me at the screen door.

Mom cocked her head. "It looks like a winch, honey. It's used to lift a heavy object." She stood there gripping her lukewarm coffee cup, staring through the bug-splattered screen.

"Heavy like what?" KK asked.

But she never got her answer because the next second Dad called out, "Come get Brownie! She's in the way." Dad had a firm grip on the retriever's collar, her nipples hanging down, her tail wick-whacking his leg. She had left her pups in the nursing box to investigate all the commotion beneath the tree. I loved her for her curiosity.

In the way of what? But I didn't ask that question. Instead, KK and I responded by corralling Brownie inside.

I clung to the aluminum grid on the inside of the screen door, my eyes fixed to the action beneath the tree. Dad looked over at me. A thin smile grew on his face, and he nodded. It was an invitation to watch. I responded by leaning my forehead on the screen and cupping my hands on the outer edges of my eyes to block out the sun. From my watching place I could see and hear everything.

Sid was still holding Rosie, her sweet face slowly chewing a mouthful of grass she had bitten off along the way. He tied her to the trunk near the cables, so close to the tree, her nose was touching the bark.

Confused, Rosie planted her hooves and pulled back from the tree. Sid placed a hand on her neck, leaning in to whisper into her left ear. It didn't work. She pulled again, hard—her eyes wild. What was happening? I wanted to run out and stop them. But Sid was whispering and rubbing her head. Then his hand went into his pocket, and he offered her a palm full of grain. The heifer eased the tension on her rope and lipped the oats.

Dad picked up the rifle casually. He walked all the way around the tree until he stood facing Rosie. He glanced over at me and nodded again. Something was wrong: His eyes were too wet, his lips too firm. And that's when it hit me. How could I have been so stupid?

I couldn't look away. It was as if my boots were nailed to the floor. Dad had me bring Rosie up here, and it felt like he was now waging war with me. Why?

As Dad approached Rosie, Sid's face was a chaos of emotion. Sid stroked the heifer's neck and said, "Aim a little above and between her eyes. If you're too low, the bullet will miss the brain, and you'll miss the kill spot."

Dad raised the rifle and I began to swipe at my cheeks.

"Steady," Sid said to Dad. "Take your time."

Suddenly, Mom's voice was loud in my ear, already pushing the door closed. "You girls shouldn't be seeing this."

"No. Leave it open." I said. I was caught in the web of the horror beneath the tree. I don't know why I wanted to watch, but Mom let go of the door.

The rifle shot exploded the silence of the mountain air, and Rosie let out a bellow of unspeakable pain. Her hind legs collapsed beneath her, forcing her into a sitting position, as she pulled at the rope that held her face to the trunk. Dad had missed the kill spot. Rosie's front legs moved in a distorted scrambling motion over the ground, attempting to flee.

Dad stood agape as Sid pulled a large hunting knife out of his belt and stuck it in the heifer's throat, severing the blood vessels and putting her out of her misery. Blood erupted from the incision, all over their boots and pouring onto the red earth at her feet. Flies gathered in a grey cloud above the bloody ground as the sound of our wailing met Dad's ears.

"Why, Dad?" I cried from behind the protective armor of the screen door. I wasn't sure which "why" I meant. There were too many: Why had I watched? Why had he made me bring Rosie to her death? Why couldn't he be like a normal father? Everything swirled in my head as I replayed the scene behind closed eyes.

Dad stepped forward as Sid hoisted Rosie up the tree. "What a little hypocrite. You like your steaks rare, don't you?"

CHAPTER SIX

That scene beneath the oak tree played through my head for months, suddenly spraying me like stray bullets. But I hardly had time to think about what I could have done, as Dad's chore list began to grow in creativity: sharpening knives and tool blades with a massive kick-wheel whetstone; watering an acre of five-gallon saplings with a weak hose in the blistering sun; driving the open-topped jeep alone loaded with alfalfa to feed cattle, horse blankets piled high on the driver's seat so I could see where I was going.

One afternoon during spring vacation, a week before my twelfth birthday, he told me to test ride Oakie, a Quarter horse he'd won gambling. Although I was excited that a new horse was here, and that Dad trusted me to be the first one to ride him, I knew nothing about the horse and I figured Dad didn't either. All I could do was try my best. The way I saw it, this job could go well, or it could land me in the hospital. Didn't matter. When Dad gave me a job, I showed up.

The warm wind lifted the branches of the Ponderosa pines and I listened to their whispers. I loved that wind voice, like a rush of river water that washed away my darker thoughts, like why Dad had become so difficult ever since he discovered the Sierras. I longed to linger with the trees. But I had this chore to do. As I walked in the direction of the old spreading oak, I passed the clothesline, loaded with T-shirts and socks too heavy to move in the afternoon breeze. Looking at my watch, I quickened my pace. I couldn't be late.

As I approached the spreading oak, I spied Dad already there, stroking Oakie's neck, his rough hand moving along the horse's chestnut withers and back, down his left hind leg, lifting and inspecting the hoof. Dad seemed pleased. I relaxed. Maybe this would go well. Maybe Oakie would have a comfortable trot and gallop and wouldn't shy at loud sounds. Maybe he wouldn't be headstrong or fight to always be at the lead; maybe he'd allow me to open and close gates while on his back, knowing all the commands, like backing up and turning around quickly. Maybe he'd be perfect.

"His past owner says Oakie's never used a bridle. . . only this hackamore." Dad jangled a jumble of leather in front of me. It looked like a horse's halter, but with more straps. "Let's see how you do with this." He handed it to me.

My hands shook. He expected me to put this contraption I'd never seen before on Oakie's head. I fumbled with the leather aided by Oakie, who smelled his familiar hackamore and nudged his graying nose forward, a gesture I took for kindness. It took me a few tries, but I finally got it on him and secured the buckle. When I stepped back, Oakie sighed and blew his soft oat breath on my skin. I smiled and looked into his eyes. How many people had he loved over the years?

I wanted to wrap my arms around his neck but Dad would have seen this as weakness. I grabbed the reins and lifted myself up into the saddle. From that vantage point, the hackamore looked just like any ordinary bridle, fitting behind his ears just so, but I frowned at the tufts of his auburn mane poking awkwardly through the straps at angles. Oakie didn't seem to mind.

I reached forward and pulled his mane from the straps, smoothing and rubbing his neck out of view of Dad. "How does a hackamore work, Dad?" It didn't have a metal bit at all, no chance of harming his soft mouth. I liked the idea of this gentler tack.

A slow smile formed on Dad's lips as he dropped his cigarette to the red dirt and gave it a crushing twist with his boot. My mouth felt dry, my stomach uneasy. This was the expression he'd worn when he'd hoisted Rosie up the oak tree and slit her belly, her blood oozing all over his feet. Now what was he going to do? His movements were graceful, almost rehearsed, as he slipped into action. I recognized the familiar condescending tilt of his head, a facial tic that meant I'd been found wanting and in need of a lesson. I settled into the saddle, awaiting instruction. I forced myself to sit tall.

Oakie jerked his head in alarm as Dad quickly stepped forward, leaning his chest against my right leg, pinning it against Oakie's side. Dad spoke with a tone that drew me in and smoothed my fears. This was the voice I loved, the voice he used as the family gathered on the back lawn in the pitch black of a summer's night, one of Dad's hands on his huge telescope the other pointing to the heavens. What had I been worrying about?

"See that? Instead of a metal bit inside the horse's mouth, there's a leather strap over his nose. When you pull the reins, pressure is applied to the most sensitive part of his face. And if you pull hard enough, it makes it difficult for the horse to breathe. Here, let me show you." His hands reached up to my face.

Dad gripped my chin with his left hand, a move that froze me to the saddle. That's when time slowed down. I saw his dirty nails, a gash on a knuckle, the little blond hairs on his callused skin. My eyes expanded as his right thumb came to rest on my left nostril.

Dad pinched my nose closed, blocking the airflow. Shocked into silence, I opened my mouth to breathe, but I did not cry out. If I had, would he have stopped?

He dug his ragged thumbnail into my flesh and slowly carved out a crescent of skin across the bridge of my nose. There was a brief look in his eyes that I'd like to think was surprise at what he was doing because in that moment he let me go. He stepped back and wiped my blood on his jeans. He cocked his head. "Now do you understand?"

My nose was on fire. Hell, I was on fire. Every part of me burned to respond. I wanted to whip him with my reins, or kick him hard in the face with the tip of my boot. Instead, I lifted my chin, aware of the exact amount of defiance he would find tolerable. Silence was my armor.

I looked down at Dad as he leaned against the trunk of the spreading oak, striking a match for the cigarette already in the grip of his lips. My stomach swirled at his casual stance, as if we had just had a nice friendly chat. Why couldn't I speak up? What would I say if I could?

I turned Oakie away from the tree, away from Dad, protecting us both. In the pasture, I swiped at the blood as my nose throbbed, but I did my job, putting Oakie through the motions of cattle work, and together we were brilliant: opening and closing gates while remaining in the saddle; backing up ten strides; loping figure eights around barrels; moving around the other horses grazing or standing in groups, their tails swatting flies, eyes half closed in the heat.

Although I tried to ignore it, occasionally blood dripped onto the saddle, a red reminder of what had taken place. But the flow soon ceased, my pain pillowed by the awareness that Oakie was my perfect companion, the kind that arrives right when you need him to.

More and more my father retreated from family life, especially if we were back home in the Bay Area. He had a secret place of worship beneath the trees in our orchard, and although he called himself an atheist, he took refuge in those trees. His temple was an old army cot dragged under a massive avocado tree he named Susan. Her branches, heavy and abundant, leaned close and enveloped him, offering protection from the world outside. His religious canon varied, but Edgar Allan Poe, Ernest Hemmingway, and John Steinbeck come to mind. In that hushed green sanctuary with his sacramental whiskey bottle, surrounded by words of power, he found peace. Throughout my childhood, other trees received his affection as well: our orchard's fruit trees. They were adored and sung to, these carefully grafted peach, apricot, and Valencia orange trees. They held his fascination like no human could, and I envied them. Eventually I grew to admire Dad's love of green things; he passed this quality on to me.

But there is one memory I have that stands in stark contrast to all the others that happened a few months after the hackamore lesson. One hot autumn Sunday afternoon I had finished my homework and was flopped on the floor of our little library inhaling the decaying pages of Black Beauty, the one with the missing dust cover and stains on page seventy-four.

Dad suddenly entered the kitchen, his boots impatient. His disdain for life had been translated into a sort of boot language, and I swear they spoke to me. I could discern different heel pressures, balances, and gaits. Dad's boots alerted me to his moods and gave me time to prepare. But right then, as they paced in the kitchen, his boots reminded me of a rodeo bull pawing in the holding pen, waiting to be released into the arena. Loud. Powerful. Wild. They instilled uncertainty and fear with just one heel-step. They commanded attention.

More noises spilled out from the kitchen while the boots rested. These sounds were friendly and inviting. Something being sliced on the cutting board; reassuring metallic clatter of measuring cups being used and then nesting; ice cubes resisting release from an ancient metal tray. Should I go help? The boots said no. They cut short the pleasurable sounds in such a way that I couldn't get up from my cushioned spot on the floor. Instead I willed myself to be invisible as his toes turned in my direction.

I am not sure what I expected, but I steeled myself for his intrusion. Would he tell me to head out into the blistering heat of the day to sieve rocks from the orchard soil for three hours? Or command that I crawl into the sweltering attic and install itchy pink insulation between the ceiling joists? More likely he'd insist that I edge the lawn with the earsplitting, rock-spitting edger, the one that had terrified me since I was six years old, when he had described what would happen if I didn't follow his orders exactly. I imagined bloody, disembodied toes as I waited for him to find me. I pretended to read.

Why had he returned so soon? My entire family sighed a collective breath every time he left for the mountains. And like freed birds when the cage door opens, we soared in his absence, laughing till we cried, harmonizing around the piano, throwing slumber parties and scrounging in the fridge for every-man-for-himself meals. But none of these experiences ever let me forget Dad's chores, his two-hour interrogation-dinner-lectures, or the embarrassment of his body stumbling out of some stranger's car, lurching sideways through the front door late at night.

Whenever Dad returned home, it was too soon. His entrance back into the house was like a cloud of noxious fumes following a bomb, and I could barely breathe. All at once I wanted Mom and my sister KK to come home, as their strengths had a way of working their magic on him. Although KK and I were affected the most by his maniacal show of power, her young age and quick wit charmed him, and she never got the worst of it. And Mom was such an actress, she could mask her emotions, flash that Hollywood smile, and say, "Oh I'm so glad I was invited to this party!" no matter what scene she was walking into.

"Fresh-squeezed orange juice?" he said, as he approached me, standing in the doorway, like a father who had repeated this scene a thousand times before. "It's fresh, from the orchard." His hazel-eyed gaze took in the pillowed scene as he bent over and his calloused hand set the glass on the floor, an inch from my own. Words gathered in my head but couldn't find their way out.

Who was this man? I was transfixed by his every move. Was this the father who carved the skin from my nose not long ago and left me bleeding? I ached for his tenderness, but at this moment, couldn't fathom what was happening. A fleeting thought that something was "wrong" with the juice ran through my mind. A little trick to catch me off guard.

I lifted the glass and sipped, orange pulp tickling my upper lip. "Thanks. . . " My voice trailed off. I wasn't prepared for this gesture of kindness. I pretended to be absorbed in Black Beauty, too intrigued by the fields of England to respond.

I didn't have one of my chronic stomachaches, the chicken pox, or even a sore throat, and yet Dad had just walked into the room and gave me a gift of juice. This was more than a little unsettling. I had padded my life full of self-protective acts when dealing with him, and suddenly—wham! No protection needed.

He turned to leave and said, "Best crop yet. Must have been all that rain." My heart soared at his attempt to share his thoughts about something so ordinary. And when he left, I heard his boots hit the kitchen linoleum. They sounded almost kind.

Why hadn't I responded? I stood up, clutching the sweating juice glass, and walked down the hallway, passing the now-empty kitchen. He was gone. Peeking inside, I saw evidence of his efforts, proof that it really had happened: a crate of oranges on the counter; the clean juicer dripping on the dish rack; a mound of peels in the compost bin.

CHAPTER SEVEN

Long after the orange juice incident I could still picture everything. I would start each day hoping Dad would repeat his kindness. I would watch and wait, analyzing his movements and the sound of his gait. I'd approach him with care as he'd announce the day's chore list. But the more I imagined it might return, the more my hope vanished. Nothing had changed.

I began to make myself scarce, waiting until he wasn't around before I moved about the house. One morning at the ranch right after school let out, I could have sworn I heard Dad's truck start up and head down the hill. I quickly slipped on my jeans and boots, excited for the summer ahead. Grabbing a banana for breakfast, I was more than a little surprised by his voice in the doorway.

"There you are." Dad fanned his face with my sixth-grade report card. "Your first chore today is to read aloud to your grandmother while I go into town. Keep reading until I return." Dad handed me *The Adventures of Tom Sawyer* and a faded copy of Webster's dictionary. "Look up all the words you don't know, and write the definitions here." He slapped a stack of binder paper on the table. "This is your ticket out into the sunshine." He looked down at my boots. "And no riding until I come back." He cuffed his truck keys off the table and let the screen door slam behind him. My chin quivered but I said nothing, my feet already sweaty in my boots.

I sank onto the old couch, the one covered in the Indian blanket, wishing I could read later in the day, when the heat of the afternoon drove us all indoors. I closed my eyes and imagined my evaporated plans. In my mind's eye I was riding Oakie along the back road, the forest to my left, the pasture to my right. I'd head into the fullness of the forest on the dusty trail, and descend to the logging road below. About half a mile up, I'd peer ahead looking for a glimpse of Hanley's cabin, which sat slumped in a small clearing not far from the Red Mine. It was like a touchstone, and helped me remember what happiness felt like.

The cabin contained my first memories of the goodness of my father, now reduced to whispery thoughts of longing. It made me think of what might have been. And I'd understand my father, or a part of him anyway. The part that loved this land. Did he know we share this love?

When Dad bought the ranch, the abandoned cabin was part of the deal. Over the years it had featured prominently in family stories, and was my favorite destination on solo rides with Oakie. Every time I stood in front of it, I remembered Dad's warning as we stood outside its front porch, Dad offering a big sweep of his arm out to his side.

"Now don't let it bother you, but old lady Hanley died in this cabin." And when we toured the tiny rooms, a few minutes later, there was her bed with a hand-sewn coverlet and a heavy indentation in the mattress, as if she'd only just gotten up moments earlier.

Rumor had it that old lady Hanley's husband had been a prospector. I imagined her dishing up venison stew out on the porch in the evenings as they listened to the mournful sound of zither music coming from somewhere on the mountain, the notes floating down like loneliness.

I liked to think it was cozy back when old lady Hanley lived there. The cabin was small and simple: One bedroom, a wood stove, a wringer washer, and a clothesline out back. It even had a primitive indoor toilet with a septic system.

Once, when I was six, we spent a summer in Hanley's cabin before moving up to the house on the hill. I don't remember how we all fit in there, but I do remember once while hanging clothes on the clothesline, Mom fell through the ground to the rusted steel septic containment tank below. She was up to her hips in human waste, the muscles in her face working hard to hide her disgust at the smell of it.

"Oh Mack!" she sang out, her arms waving huge windshield wiper arcs in the air, as if she were late for the opera and was flagging down a cab. I remember Dad's laugh as he bent in half, slapping his thigh while she pleaded for help.

But now another family lived there: the Gallos. There were seven of them, five small children and their parents. Dad was the one who had invited them to stay until they got their feet on the ground, but over the last few months he'd taken to calling them names: drifters, good-for-nothings, squatters.

———

"Honey? Are you ready to read?" Grandma's voice interrupted my thoughts, reminding me I had a reading job to do. I stood up, gathering *Tom Sawyer*, the dictionary, and the stack of binder paper into my arms.

Although I loved my grandparents, it was unsettling when they visited the ranch. They seemed so out of place, pacing throughout the day with nothing to do, hovering like ghosts. They were Dad's parents, but he never went out of his way for them like Mom did. She was the one who called them every morning, and the one who'd suggested their visit.

I felt I needed to protect my grandparents, too, from discovering what I already knew, that my father didn't give a hoot about them, and I knew exactly what that felt like. But when I walked into my parents' bedroom and my eyes fell on Grandma's impish grin as she sat in the simple slat-back wooden chair, her bottom overflowing the capacity of the seat, I just had to smile. Like my grandfather, she was always quietly challenging Dad's punishments or declarations, softening their blow. This morning we were like cell-mates, stuck in the room until the jailor returned, and I knew Grandma was going to attempt to make my 'sentence' something good to remember.

Grandma's grey waist-length hair was braided and pinned on her head, framing her face. Her belly, round and forgiving, served as a perch for her vein-riddled hands. I could see she wanted, even needed, this task of listening to me. It gave her something to do. I plopped at the foot of the bed, and pointed my feet in the direction of the windows.

Grandma sat opposite me, under a thin rectangular window. Through it I could make out the very top of an oak tree, where black-throated warblers were flitting from branch to branch, their white tail feathers a soft contrast to the gnarled branches they preferred. As I read the opening passages of *Tom Sawyer*, Grandma closed her eyes in the warmth of the room, smiling at Mark Twain's words and my attempts to make them come alive.

Under her watch, I scaled a jagged ravine of vocabulary: diffident, alacrity, portentous. Upbraid, sublimity, derision. Miscreant, phrenological, conflagration. With each new word a moan, a grab of the dictionary, a definition copied carefully in my very best cursive.

I realized the assignment could have been a lot worse.

Dad could have added math problems to the chore. Certainly my report card had mentioned that disaster too. At school it was painful to decipher what was written on the blackboard or page. At times, numbers and letters exchanged places, or dropped off the page altogether. Teachers re-taught, sometimes patiently, other times not, but I just couldn't get it.

I didn't dare tell my parents of my struggles, but at report card time Dad would shake his head as he loomed over my grades and Mom would force a smile, pray and redouble her effort to help me with my homework.

Grandma found the "dictionary business" tedious, and miraculously for me, did away with it, preferring to tell me the meaning of the words herself. Occasionally Mom would walk into the room and add to Grandma's definitions.

They'd joke and use the words in sentences, securing my understanding.

"Can you tell felicity has something to do with happiness? Why, you can't even say the word without smiling. Just try!"

"Felicity," I repeated, grinning as the last bit of the word fell from my lips.

"And felicity means blissful happiness, honey. You know, I once had a friend by that name. There never was a happier girl." Grandma smiled and nodded for me to continue.

As the morning wore on and I saw them relish the glory of each passage, admiring Mark Twain's humor and word choice, I wondered if I would ever be like them—comfortable, even playful with words. Would I ever be a great reader?

How many times had I been mesmerized by their voices? By Mom sitting in the front of my classroom, a small well-worn pile of poetry books in her lap, as her voice painted wild and wonderful pictures for my classmates.

Or by Grandma, reciting poems in Scottish dialect from the comfort of her easy chair. "Here's another from Bobby Burns you might like." And we'd giggle because she'd pronounce Burns like Bearrrrns, hugging the "r" to the roof of her mouth, like melted chocolate.

Ninety minutes later my voice was giving out and my resolve to complete this chore was waning. I looked into Mom's face, hoping she'd put an end to this, but there wasn't even a glimmer of exhaustion in her smile. I took a breath and scanned the next sentence, spying yet another new word, neon in its uniqueness: f-a-t-i-g-u-e. I closed my eyes and imagined writing it on a big blackboard.

"Fah-tee-gew," I sounded out.

Grandma looked at Mom out of the corner of her eye, my mispronunciation seeming to disturb her composure. "Fatty-gew! Well if that doesn't beat all!" The giggling burst from her mouth and she turned away, trying to smother it with curve of her hand.

"It's pronounced fah-teeg, honey," Mom said, suddenly substituting for Grandma. "It means exhaustion."

I slammed the book closed and walked to the window that looked out into the forest, too embarrassed to turn around and see their faces. I stared out to the towering wall of Ponderosa pines and noticed an unsettling change had come over them. They were altered, diminished somehow. Was it my eyes, or. . .

"Do you smell smoke?" I spun around toward Mom. She lowered her chin, fixing me with a frown, as if I were making this up. I scrunched my nose up. "I'm not kidding. Don't you smell it?"

Grandma unclasped her hands from her lap and stood. She joined me at the window and put her hand on my shoulder. "Why Margot, she's right. There is smoke out there."

I don't recall the volunteer fire department's old siren winding its way through the hills signaling concern, or neighbors calling to find out if we could see what was going on. Just the mountain's silence as we walked outside and stood in the driveway, watching wave after wave of ghostly smoke roll over on itself, blurring the lines of the stables like gauze.

KK burst outside. "Mom, shouldn't we leave?" Her voice was lowered to a whisper as if asking herself the question. She backed up to the siding, apart from us, as if distancing herself from Mom. For some time now KK had grown distrustful of our mother's lack of common sense, but she had learned to frame her complaints as questions. I looked at her and nodded agreement, as she wiped beads of sweat from her upper lip. I imagined the tongues of flame quickly swallowing up the trees, devouring the distance between us. At the same time, I trusted that if it really came to it, if the trees really were a wall of flames Mom would drive us to safety.

Grandma grabbed Mom's arm. "D'you think it's close, Margot?"

Mom cleared her throat. "I think it's time to do some thinking about this." Mom's word *thinking* was her way of saying it was time to pray. Since my grandmother was also a Christian Scientist, she quickly agreed and they retreated into the bedroom, leaving KK and me standing there in the smoke.

I knew the fire was still a ways from reaching us, but KK's fear made me want to race down the mountain to make sure. I wanted to bring the news back to her, to tell her it would be okay, but there was no way I could leave now— not with Mom and Grandma holed up in the bedroom, and Dad out of yelling distance. What if I was wrong and the fire spread to our house while I was gone?

I heard Oakie whinny nervously, unable to see his surroundings, and I realized the grey fingers of smoke were reaching for everything I loved.

KK sighed. "I can't breathe out here." Her tone had lost some of the fear, like she had been puzzling it over in her head as she watched the sky, but her body was heavy with disappointment.

I nodded. I looked over at the stables, a two-minute walk away, and knew exactly what I had to do. "Be right back," I said to the screen door that had just slammed.

It took me one minute to fast-walk the short distance to the corral, where Sid was shaking oats in a bucket to coax a horse into a stall. He looked up as I approached.

"The horses ain't in any danger yet—just stirred up, that's all." He shook the bucket again.

I stepped forward, brushing my bangs out of my eyes. "Shouldn't we move them out?"

"Naw. We're okay up here." Sid pointed with his free hand down the hill. "The firemen have been down there for quite some time now. I bet it'll all be over soon." How was he so sure? "You head on up to your family and tell 'em not to worry." But I didn't budge.

"Go on. Up here, fires are just a part of life."

It wasn't until late that afternoon, when the smoke had dissipated a bit, that Dad returned. He parked his red truck under the bough of a Ponderosa pine, as far from the front door as he could get. His window was down and I watched from behind the screen door as the dappled sun came through the windshield and illuminated his ruddy forehead. He leaned over and lit a Viceroy, sucking in the smoke. His free arm extended out of the cab and hung there, resting on the warm metal of the door.

He said nothing when he entered the house, just walked into the kitchen and set down some groceries. All of us trailed into the room, Mom in the lead.

"It was pretty exciting around here, Mack." Mom's voice was cheery as she put her hand on his shoulder.

"You mean the smoke?" The cigarette bobbed in his mouth as he talked.

"Of course!" KK's impatience came with a hand on her hip. I loved that she said this, but knew if it had been me, he would have stopped and slowly turned, leveling his eyes on me, or worse.

He smiled at her outburst, "Oh, that's just old Hanley's shack."

"Oh Mack, not Hanley's cabin. . . " Mom's face crumpled.

I broke in before mom could finish. "Were the kids there?" I could imagine all five of them running from the flames.

Dad shrugged. "Looks like it was time to move on, 'cuz nobody was home. My guess is he got a job somewhere and just forgot that the beans were on the stove when they drove away. Now c'mon, let's get dinner on the table." As I moved into the kitchen to help shuck corn, I couldn't help but notice the smell of smoke on his clothes. Had Dad set the fire to get them to leave?

CHAPTER EIGHT

I fell asleep that night wondering about the Gallos. Where had they gone? The next morning I awoke a little after 5:00, my head mired in dark thoughts. I knew what I had to do. I had to see for myself, but couldn't tell anyone where I was going. I slipped into my riding clothes and left, putting my boots on outside.

Oakie was surprised to see me so early, but lifted his head when I approached, happy to comply with my urgency for an early morning ride. I took the back driveway, away from the house that bordered the forest. Nobody would see me there. About half a mile from home, I saw the gutted skeletons of trees, curving inward like black parentheses, leaning toward the destruction.

Horses are honest about change. They don't like it one bit, and they let you know it. Some riders get tense at this display, getting hard on the horse. But allowing Oakie an honest reaction didn't seem like a big deal. He was an older cattle horse, and had seen a lot of drama in his life. He could handle it.

I patted his neck, and talked softly as he walked, agreeing that the forest looked scary. I talked about the smells, the burnt trees, the horrific loss of nature. I sounded calm, but when we arrived, I too was struck by the emptiness. The cabin was reduced to a small scorched foundation.

I could make out part of the woodstove, flipped onto its back, and a cast iron kettle, which had landed nearby as if to keep it company. The only other thing I could see that held memories was the rust-stained claw-foot tub, still sitting thirty feet from the house under a pine tree branch, intended for outdoor bathing. I thought about those hot afternoons long ago when KK and I would splash in our "pool" under the shade of the Ponderosas, and I'd wondered at the magnificence of our luck.

I walked Oakie around the backside of the charred clearing, behind the trees that bordered it. I'm not sure what I was looking for, but I felt compelled to look for something. Maybe one other thing to prove that the Gallos had been here? Ten minutes into my search, I saw a soft paleness against the dark greens and browns of the mountain misery and bracken. I clucked for Oakie to move closer, but in the end I climbed out of the saddle to investigate.

It was a baby doll, its face melted forward, one eye sunk into its cheek. Then I remembered a day about six months before, when Dad and I rode by on our way to a remote trail. As we approached the cabin, a toddler was sitting on the porch with a baby doll in her arms. She had been singing, but the moment she saw us she stopped. She stared at the ground. Was this melted doll hers? Where was she? Was she hurt? As I placed it at the base of a protective Ponderosa pine, my sadness grew to encompass not only the children, but also their mother who'd lived here, who over the last six months we'd frequently seen waiting with her children in their rusty car outside the local tavern, while we waited for our father to come out too. I thought about Dad and Mr. Gallo escaping from their families, unaware of the damage they caused.

It was getting late. I rode back to the stables, and was brushing Oakie down when a white truck drove up our driveway and parked under the oak tree. I didn't pay much attention, just assumed it was someone for Dad, or maybe someone curious about the fire. But when I put Oakie into his stall and turned toward the house, Dad was standing near the front door, in the shadow of a man I had never seen before. I had been worried how I would explain my early morning absence, and was grateful for this distraction. Perhaps Dad hadn't even noticed I had been gone.

The stranger had an open face and an apologetic manner, and was leaning toward my father, squinting his eyes as he talked, as if he was puzzling things out, sorry he had to trouble Dad so early in the morning.

KK was standing in the side yard, hidden by the bulk of Mom's Impala, listening to their conversation. I snuck over to her, my eyes wide, knowing she'd fill me in. I looked over at Dad and the stranger, not twenty paces from where we were hiding. KK whispered that he was the captain of the fire department, and that he'd come up here to ask Dad a few questions.

The next words the captain spoke made my breath catch. "Sir, I don't think so. In fact, there's evidence to suggest the fire was set." He turned away from Dad and reached into the cab of his truck for a pen, talking loudly over his shoulder. "Know anyone who had a grudge against them?"

"I can't help you there. They kept to themselves." My dad's voice sounded alien, filled with concern.

"So there was never any trouble down there? No arguing? No teenage son causing problems, or. . . "

Dad's eyes darted in the direction of where the cabin used to be. "No, no. The kids were little. That wife of his couldn't possibly have kept her eyes on all of them."

Dad straightened to his full height and put a hand on

his hip, little blasts of air exiting his nose in short pulses, his signature chuckle. The captain had no idea what this meant, but I did. Dad was done with the questions. He was now in control of this conversation, and was laughing at Mrs. Gallo for her incompetence. Dad's next words came slowly. "Think about it. With five kids under the age of eight all over the place, it's certainly possible there was an accident."

The captain looked toward the blackened trees, and scratched his chin. He folded his arms across his chest, twisting his top wrist to peek at his watch. He nodded, but said nothing. What was happening? I looked over at KK, but she was staring at Dad.

The captain's lips were pinched together, his pen scratching the pad of paper, forming more words than my father had said. Dad leaned closer, squinting as the captain's scrawled. The captain looked up, lowering his voice. "Sir, how had the Gallos come to live on your property?"

My dad blew a puff of air through his closed lips. "Mr. Gallo had a real sad story, and it got to me. It would you too. Lost his job, had too many kids, a wife with no skills, and no money in the bank."

"Did he mention where he had worked?" The captain's Adam's apple bobbed.

"Never said. Labor of some kind, I'd guess. I let him stay in the cabin because that's what you do, don't you? Lend a hand when a guy needs it? I told him he could pay rent when he got his feet back on the ground. He was real appreciative when I offered the place. Even bought me a drink." Dad grinned at the memory.

The captain cleared his throat and checked his watch again. He seemed to have come to a decision. "Well, since the fire was on your property, and you don't plan on filing a complaint, I believe we're done here." He shook dad's hand and then tucked the paperwork into the cab of his truck.

Dad lit a Viceroy and gripped it between his thumb and index finger, flicking the free fingers in dismissal to the departing truck. He rocked back on his boot heels and chuckled softly as he walked to his own truck, and headed in the direction of fire's devastation.

I couldn't stop thinking about the fire. Was it my imagination, or was Dad even more disgruntled than before? A week after the fire, Mom and I were down at the stable getting ready for a long trail ride together. Dad called from his truck as he headed out down the hill. "You'll ride Noches today. He needs to stretch his legs."

I nodded but fear crept into my happiness. Noches was a spirited black gelding and I wondered if this was such a great idea. A dark thought nagged at my gut that Dad was trying to scare me, but I pushed it aside. He'd never do that with Mom on the ride. I helped Mom into the saddle. She was riding Comanche, a gentle grey oaf of a horse, whom she adored.

Since I'd never ridden Noches before, each movement he made was a lesson in temperament and skill—both his and mine. I soon grew comfortable and learned to anticipate what he'd do next, in the way I did with humans. In the saddle I also knew I would discover something about what his previous owner was like—heavy handed, fearful, kind, or abusive—past horsemanship always played out during the course of a long ride. It said a lot about a person.

As you descend the brush-covered mountain to get to the logging road, you first have to cross the drainage ditch. Each horse has its own special way to do this, and Noches attacked it as if it were a wide rushing stream. It felt like we flew over it. Now on the other side of the ditch, safe on the dirt road, he began to prance sideways, ears forward, eager for freedom. I pulled him up, fearing this ride might be a bit more stressful than I had anticipated. I turned around to watch Mom who was following right behind.

Mom's horse Comanche lowered his head at the drainage ditch, and sniffed it. Comanche was a huge appaloosa, calm and sure, and was at heart a bit lazy. He slowly lifted one front leg, and placed it across the ditch to the road. The rest of his body followed in one massive lumbering movement, while Mom bobbed back and forth, a mixture of surprise and humor on her lips. It was then that I noticed the odd tilt of Mom's saddle. "Your cinch is loose, Mom. Let me check it."

"Oh, you old hoo-hah!" Mom said, wagging a finger at Comanche. He was famous for taking a deep breath and holding it while his saddle was being cinched, then letting it out when a rider got into the saddle. This made him much more comfortable during the ride, but if not caught in time, the loose cinch could prove deadly.

I could still hear Sid teaching me this lesson on a pack trip to Thousand Island Lakes, as he squatted on the ground, frying trout for our dinner. "There was this new fella who joined us at the old ranch in Oklahoma. He was real proud of his ability to work fast at sortin' cattle. And the boss encouraged him. The rest of us took no mind of his showing off, him being young and all. It's a real shame what happened to him that day.

"It was a hot afternoon, and we were sortin' calves from cows, for market. The work was tiring, as we'd chase a fleeing calf, and then spin on a dime to chase another. But this boy showed no sign of exhaustion as he dug his heels into his mare and moved her in and out of the herd, like silk." Sid paused, deep in the memory.

I looked at him huddled over the makeshift camp stove, a battered spatula in his hand, as he lifted the edges of the trout to check for color. Little bits of cornmeal fell off the fish and into the sizzling fat. He seemed to be searching for something. When he continued, his voice was resigned to the telling.

"Never once saw him check his cinch. And he didn't rest his horse neither. Then it happened. Frustrated by an ornery little bull-calf who had spent the morning fleeing capture, the boy lost his temper and gave chase, bursting after it at full speed. As he came up alongside its flank, the calf jerked to the left, in the direction of his mama. That boy pulled so hard on the left rein, his saddle slipped sideways. They were at a full gallop and with each pound of hooves, his saddle inched further and further down the right side of his mare's chest until the boy was upside down and staring up at his mare's body.

"We heard his scream, but by the time we got there, the mare's hooves had struck his head, splitting his skull wide open. He was dead alright, but caught up in the saddle, just dangling there. Terrified, the mare tried to lose him, but lost her balance and fell hard over the boy's body, shattering her front leg. It was me who ended up shooting her, and none of it was her fault. Felt mighty upset about that."

———

Now Noches whinnied at Mom's approach, and I climbed off the saddle to tighten my cinch, and then tackled Comanche's. His big grey head swung around and nosed my arm as I tightened the strap around his belly.

He lipped my sleeve, and I nudged his soft nose away. "Knock it off, mister. There's no way I'm letting anything bad happen to us today."

I was about to climb back into the saddle, but the beauty of this spot stopped me in my tracks. Mom's eyes were closed, as they often were in places of beauty, but mine were wide open. The sudden call of a red-tailed hawk underscored my love for this place, with its wild loneliness, and I wondered, not for the first time, what it would be like to have this as my backyard every day. I felt pang of guilt as I thought it, thinking of my best friend back in Saratoga. I missed her giggles and how her father made me laugh at their dinner table. I was suddenly homesick.

I patted Noches' neck and climbed into the saddle, remembering a conversation I'd overheard down at the stables between Dad and Sid the day before.

"I heard Dad say he wants to move here," I told Mom. I clucked at Noches and we started off down the snaking road.

"Oh honey, we don't need to live here to love it." Mom's voice held a certain exhaustion I couldn't explain. "There is no opera, no symphony, no ballet. . . and then there are the schools."

"What's wrong with the schools?" My mind conjured up a rundown building with bullies roaming the playground, kicking little kids and smoking cigarettes.

"Well, they're not what I want for you." I was relieved to be lifted from my schoolyard nightmare. But I felt torn, too, because I understood Dad's desire—to wake up every day to the rustle of the wind through the pines and the haunted calls of the red-tailed hawk. If I was honest, it was my desire too, but I knew what the city meant to Mom. This would be a mighty fight, one I didn't want to be part of, and I wasn't sure who would win.

Perhaps noting the tension in Mom's voice, Noches moved into a trot, and I let him use up a bit of his energy. His trot was silky but given to sudden head turns, as if he were watching the movement of birds.

Knowing Mom wasn't a big fan of Comanche's jarring trot, I called back to her, "Want to gallop?"

Mom came along side of me, with a thousand watt smile. "Sure!" She tapped her heels lightly on Comanche's side.

His long legs shot forward, taking the lead as we galloped around the curves of the Sierras, shrouded in hardy pines, scrub oaks and madrones. Noches was small but competitive. I relaxed and trusted, letting him have his head. His neck bobbed impatiently to move out ahead of Comanche. Like a panther, in one fluid movement, he sprang in front of Comanche and remained there weaving around the curves of the mountain, putting his ears back whenever Comanche came too close.

As we rounded a bend in the road, I saw a jumble of huge stationary machinery and trees, evidence of a logging job in progress. This being a weekend, there were no men or trucks around, but I instinctively slowed down.

Mom screamed. I spun around, my eyes absorbing the chaos. She was on her back on a rough mound of rock protruding from the ground, her limbs spread out in contorted confusion, the heel of her right boot where her toes should be. Comanche was stumbling about, not ten feet from Mom's head, punctuating the sudden stillness with his whinny.

I suspect he had been galloping when he stumbled on logging debris. I moved toward him in the hope of blocking him from accidentally stepping on her. I couldn't yell, or I'd make things worse, but his proximity to her head terrified me. As if reading my thoughts, Comanche's legs came to rest. His body shook as he extended his big neck toward Mom, eyes wide, as if surprised she was there on the ground and not on his back, his warm breath falling on her like an apology.

"Honey!" Mom rasped a breathy croak. She tried to move her hands to push herself up, but she couldn't. I leapt off of Noches. Grabbing the reins I tried to make him walk with me over to Mom, but he pulled back, bobbing his head in refusal. I wanted to drop the reins and run to her. She was mumbling something and I wanted to hear the words. I wanted to hold her. But if a let Noches go, he'd bolt for sure. Dad would kill me if a horse came back without the rider.

"Come on Noches," I said, my voice was creepily soft, but in my head I was screaming the words, thwacking his rump to move forward. Ten feet to my left, Comanche's head lifted at my voice, his reins now dangling on the ground. My heart sank as I realized I needed to somehow grab them too, and I had to do it fast before it dawned on him he was free. I clucked softly, and marveled as both horses moved toward me. I reached out and grabbed Comanche's reins. We were now a trio.

When I got close enough to see Mom's face, I was shattered with guilt. Why had I suggested the gallop? She wasn't a strong rider. We should have stopped sooner. What was I thinking?

"What happened, Mom?"

It was hard to understand her. "Tripped. . . " Her voice frightened me, and I moved closer. I could see a ragged edge on the top of the rock she was laying on. It had sliced through her shirt, but I saw no blood. I knew she was in pain.

"Are you okay?" It was a stupid question. But what else could I say? As a Christian Scientist, would she ever admit she was hurt? She had endured dental drills, childbirth, and migraines without medical help. But her face was grey and I knew I needed to get help, no matter what she said. But how could I leave her there on the ground?

"Mom, there's a tree stump behind you. Would you like me to help you lean against it?" I motioned to the spot a foot from her head.

A groan came from her throat, like a sick beast. "Get . . . your. . . dad." For a split second, I recoiled at the idea of her needing him for anything. But terror seized my body. I'd do anything for her.

"Okay!" I looped Comanche's reins over a branch and Noches and I tore out of the clearing. It seemed to take hours to do the fifteen minutes back to the ranch. I galloped up the driveway, to the ranch house at the top of the hill, repeatedly calling "Dad!"

He must have heard my shouts, because when I crested the hill, Dad was standing outside smoking a cigarette. "Where's your mother?"

I sobbed the words out, my message chopped and garbled. "Comanche tripped. Mom fell onto a rock. She can't get up."

He dropped his cigarette on the ground and crushed it with a boot. "Tie up the horse and get in the jeep." Dad revved the engine and suddenly there was a scatter of gravel on asphalt as heavy hooves topped the hill to the house. It was Comanche, galloping with abandon, eyes wide with confusion. He stopped when he got to the oak tree.

"God dammit!" Dad jumped from the Jeep and moved to where Comanche stood, exhausted, his chest heaving. How could I be so stupid? I had just thrown Comanche's reins over a branch when I fled to get help. Had he trampled Mom on his way out of the clearing? I knew Dad was wondering the same thing as his meaty hands secured Comanche to the tree, making a show of tugging the rope securely, highlighting my inadequacy.

We pulled into the loggers' clearing five minutes later, and the sight of Mom struck me cold. She hadn't moved, her face now as white as lilies.

"Jesus! What kind of a daughter are you?" Dad turned to stare at me. "Stay here."

Dad stepped around fallen trees and stumps, squatting by her head. His position hid her face from me and all I could see was a one-sided conversation as his head nodded, shook, and argued. He jogged back to the jeep. "Stay with your mother, but don't touch her. I'm calling an ambulance." Dad peeled off into the forest to make the phone call from the ranch house.

When Dad drove up followed by the ambulance, he turned and pointed up the hill. "Walk home and stay with your little sister. We're taking your mother to Amador County Hospital."

I wanted to scream, "No!" and jump in the ambulance with Mom, but I knew better. I nodded and started the hike back to the ranch.

It was after midnight when Dad returned from the hospital, his barrel-chested silhouette appearing in the doorway to the bedroom I shared with KK. I could smell the whiskey before he even spoke.

"Dad?" I whispered from the top bunk.

He put a hand on the wall to steady himself and slurred the news. "Your mom's a cripple now. You proud of yourself?"

CHAPTER NINE

We visited Mom in the hospital, Dad having dropped us off outside, preferring not to join us. Walt, KK and I serenaded Mom with a guitar, something the nurses strictly forbade—but we didn't care. I can still see her smile as we sang the Beatles' song, "Help!"

And I soon realized it was a good thing that before her accident she had spent a great deal of time on her bed praying and reading the newspaper, because that's all she got to do once she returned home.

We'd rushed outside when Dad brought her back to the ranch one sweltering afternoon, and we trailed them both down the hallway as he laid her on the bed. I brought her ice water and the bedpan, and she never complained about anything. Once, when she patted my hand I was relieved to discover her skin was still cold, even when it was ninety degrees outside. I loved that about her. Her coolness. Sometimes I read her a get-well card or part of a Nancy Drew mystery, but mostly she lay there alone as Dad's chore lists grew.

One morning as I sat in the rocker telling Mom a joke, I heard Dad's boots shuffling toward the bedroom. He stepped inside and flipped a dishtowel over his shoulder, the color of a bull-fighter's cape. "You're needed in the kitchen. You're canning today."

I looked over at Mom as if she would ask me to remain, but I knew better. I got up to follow Dad out, my thighs stuck to the upholstered chair. Canning in this heat—was he kidding?

When I walked into the kitchen, the stench of tomatoes hit me full force. I clapped a hand over my nose, willing the nausea to go away. Tomatoes. . . really?

Something was wrong with me, that's what Dad always said. Everyone was wild about tomatoes—especially right off the vine, so Dad decided I was simply ornery, and he was on a mission to make me love them too. I had happily weeded and hoed the tomato plants, tried bites of the beautiful globes ripe in the sun, and had been forced to eat them at the dinner table while everyone watched. But each time, my throat would seize and I'd managed to spit them into my napkin.

"Hot stuff—stand clear!" Dad lifted the boiling tomatoes off the burner, his boots moving in a practiced heel-toe step as he strode to the kitchen sink, steam rising into his face, moistening his ruddy cheeks. He seemed to relish all of this, the bubbling, simmering heat of the day.

I had first noticed Dad's thing about heat while helping him in the kitchen about six months ago, back when cooking with him was almost fun. That night we'd been preparing a complicated dinner and running late. Dad had barked demands as I ping-ponged around the kitchen, trying to keep up with him. His goal was to make multiple dishes and have them all come out at the same time, and I had enjoyed the rush of excitement at the challenge and my small successes.

The strange part began right before we called everyone to the dinner table, when Dad clapped his hands and shouted, "Last job—look alive." He marched to the oven and pulled the door open, lifting his lips back into a wide smile. My eyes narrowed. He looked like one of those guys on TV, demonstrating the latest GE appliances. He reached an arm into the hot cave of the oven and plucked out a fat potato. The escaping heat wafted into the kitchen, lifting wisps of his hair like sea anemones. What was he doing?

"Remember now, you need to put one spud on each plate." The potato was sitting there like a hot rock in his hand, but he didn't flinch. He didn't toss them back and forth between his hands. It was like he had hot pads for fingers.

Any normal Dad would have pierced the potato with a fork. A simple job. One stab and it would be plopped into a serving dish. Repeat a bunch of times, and voila! A dish of potatoes to take to the table. But not Dad.

"Catch!" He cupped the potato in his right hand.

"Catch?" A trickle of sweat ran down my back. That's when Dad threw the potato underhand, as if we were playing on the lawn. My mind went blank. What would he do if I dropped it?

I stepped forward and it hit my chest, then bounced down into my cupped hands. It had split open and I gasped at the pain of it, tossing the potato toward the table, but missing it altogether. It landed with a thud on the floor. I grabbed a napkin and squatted down to clean up the tight mounds of brown skin torn from the steaming flesh, like volcanic islands at my feet. My shoulders prepared for Dad's anger as I blew on my hands, the burn of potato still on my skin.

But Dad didn't erupt. Was this just a joke? A little fun between us as the dinner preparations came to an end?

I looked over and saw him reach for another, and knew he wasn't finished.

"Incoming!" I jumped up as the second spud came flying at my head. I moved and it landed with a heavy smack into my outstretched hands, the surprise making my knees lock.

"Dad, please don't. Slow down." Slow down? What about "Dad, stop it!" But I didn't dare say it. Besides, he wasn't listening.

The potatoes kept coming like bombs. Fastballs, curve-balls, anything-to-keep-me-on-my-toes balls. Dad smiled though all of it—delighted when I caught one, laughing at my clumsy misses, each of his responses forcing me to the unthinkable—that my father was trying to hurt me. That he wasn't normal. Not even close.

He stood with his chest thrust forward, thumbs hooked into his belt loops, watching my every move. His eyes held all the light in the room as he tipped his head back and howled with glee. I wanted to throw a steaming potato at him. I'd hit his face and the potato would split across his nose and singe his ruddy face, leaving its mark. I pushed aside the image—I needed all my energy to anticipate the next curveball.

The final potato was thrown around his back, and his wild grin when I caught it, exploded. "That's the ticket!" The effect was immediate. With his simple praise I realized I wanted to catch more potatoes.

The smell of the tomatoes and the heat of the day brought me back to my senses. I was still standing in the kitchen, sur-rounded by canning jars and bubbling lids with the tomato stench all around me. What was it about the sweat gathering on the back of Dad's thick neck that made me look away? I could hear my brothers playing cards in the living room.

Why didn't the boys ever have to help in the kitchen? And where was KK?

"Royal Flush!" Don hooted as cards fanned onto the table.

"Dammit!" Walt's chair scraped the old wood floor and he appeared in the kitchen, fanning his face. "Jesus, it's hot. Get me a Coke." His words were for me.

I sighed and opened the fridge, grabbing a Coke for His Majesty. Oh, the sudden chill of it! I wanted to pour it over my head.

Dad barked, "Get out of the kitchen unless you want to be put to work."

I backed away from Dad, as far away as possible, and suddenly KK came into the room, her hair a scrambly mess. Dad smiled at her and gesticulated toward the pot of boiled tomatoes. His face glowed, like he had birthed the lot of them, one thumb hanging from a belt loop, his chest thrust out. "Let's get to these tomatoes, girls. The First thing you'll do is—"

"Dad, I feel sick." KK 's voice was weird as she put a hand over her stomach and bent forward. Was she faking? Was I was going to be stuck here doing this by myself? KK groaned and I bent down to look at her face, pale as paper.

"Jesus H Christ. Enough interruptions!" Dad's boots scraped the linoleum as he pivoted toward us.

But right then, KK's cough came from deep in her gut, more bark than human, and I followed her as she lurched for the bathroom. The least I could do was lift the toilet seat and hold back her hair. But Dad gripped my arm. "Stay here. Your mother can take care of her." Had he forgotten that Mom was bedridden? All she could do was pray. It dawned on me that even barfing and all alone, KK was the lucky one.

"She'll be fine. Let's get to it." Dad pivoted to the stove

and I quickly wiped my eyes with the back of my hand. We stood facing his steaming pot of scalding tomatoes. The effort to listen to him was unbearable. I wanted to help KK. I wanted to be riding. I wanted out of this damned kitchen.

A bird's call was all it took, and my attention moved outdoors, where the Sierras sang me to life. Although the details of the trees were blurred by the steam on the window glass, it didn't matter. I knew them by heart—the blending of greens and browns was enough to remind me of their limbs and leaves, their needles and trunks. It was as if I could smell the perfume of pine, mountain misery and warm red earth. I could hear the wind whispering in trees, calling me to them. They were my protectors. They would shield me from the heat, their branches reaching far beyond imagining.

Dad cleared his throat, jerking me back to the hazy heat of the kitchen. He was midsentence. I hadn't heard anything. Had he noticed?

". . . You need to remove the skin before canning, and to do this, you boil the tomatoes first." He reached one calloused hand into the still sweltering pot and scooped out a red blob, tossing it from palm to palm. "Your job is to squeeze the skin off. It's easiest when the tomato is still pretty warm."

I looked at the tomato in Dad's hands. It looked like a little head. He squeezed his fingers around it, and the pulp fell into a bowl in the sink. "See how simple it is?" His right palm held the glossy skin as bits of it clung to his fingers. Dad shook his hand and the skin plopped into the sink. "Now you try."

"But it's still boiling hot." I looked up into his face.

"Nah. You'll get used to it."

━━━━━━━━

Life back home in Saratoga carried the weight of everything that had happened that summer in the Sierras. I began to do things I didn't quite understand. Strange, compulsive things that somehow softened reality and made me responsible for things going well: tapping the doorframe three times before entering a room; holding my breath for exactly seven seconds before getting out of bed; doing a perfect double pirouette in front of the refrigerator before allowing myself to open it.

And then there were the baths. It all started casually, one Sunday evening in the middle of a fierce storm. The wail of the wind lifted the rain and slammed it sideways, a thousand frenzied fingers pummeling the window. I loved the power of the wind, whether whispery soft while riding a trail, or like tonight—exquisitely frightening, her three-toned howl preparing to throw the town into darkness.

I twisted the hot water faucet, and a cascade surged into the tub. Grabbing my Smokey the Bear bubble bath from his perch on the tub, I poured the yellow fluid into his ranger-hat cap and drizzled it like melted butter into the water. Instantly, frothy islands sprang up like magical kingdoms, moving on the surface like the continental drift, joining with others, their puffy iridescence expanding upward.

The thought of my unfinished geography homework flashed before me and I tried to push it aside, but the all-too-familiar stab of guilt sat hard in my stomach. Recently, I'd been unable to concentrate on any assignment for very long. I imagined my smart classmates pouring over their homework right after dinner, a thesaurus at their side, their parents interested in their assignments.

The wind's caterwaul rattled the window. I shivered and scrunched the small rug under my toes, savoring the soft familiar yarn. I exhaled loudly. Dad was in the Sierras. It was easier to breathe when he was gone. I dipped a finger into the tub. No way was it hot enough. I had come up with the brilliant idea of adding boiling water to the bath.

I slipped down the hallway to retrieve the simmering

pot off the stove, hoping Mom and KK wouldn't notice. Hearing Andy Griffith's voice and their responding laughter, I relaxed. I wanted to join in their fun, but I had something important to do. If the bath was hot enough, I could shut out the world. I could prove I was strong.

I closed the bathroom door, and tipped the entire contents of the pot into the tub. The steam hit my face, enveloping me in its all-encompassing moisture. The mirror went opaque, the way I liked it. Maybe when it cleared I would be different.

As I stared at the bubbles, I imagined the scalding water waiting just underneath the surface. The longer I stared, the more it taunted, "You think you can take this? Bah! You can't even get in the damned tub."

Once, I'd asked Mom if I could be harmed by heat—and she had said, "Pain is an illusion—like fear. Only God's love is real." Was she right? I had thought about the Life Magazine sitting in the living room, with pictures of Biafran refugees. There was one of a little girl, perhaps four years old. She was alone in the dirt, more skeleton than human, looking out at the horizon, waiting for the return of her family. Her patience ripped at my chest. Mom and I had sat on the couch together as she had read the article aloud.

I couldn't take my eyes off of the child. It was the first time I'd seen such outrage. How could famine be possible? I thought God loved everybody. I wanted to reach into the picture and put her on my lap. I wanted to feed her.

"But if she's starving, why is her stomach sticking out?" I searched Mom's eyes for the truth.

"She has no food, honey. That's just a trick the body plays." It wasn't really an answer.

As Mom read, my body leaned into hers, our positions reverting to the comfort of a thousand bedtimes. She skipped the medical details, keeping her voice soft—as if she held a promise of happiness. I knew what she was thinking: If we just anchored ourselves in the goodness of God, none of this would have happened. I wanted to believe her. But I believed in the goodness of God, and I felt pain. It came with the thwack of leather on bare skin, the tearing of flesh from a nose, or when you dipped your hand in a steaming pot of tomatoes. And yet, Mom wove such a soothing web of love the very idea of turning my back on her was unimaginable.

———

I knew the bath was going to hurt. That's what I was counting on. Enduring the heat wasn't just some silly game—it was a brilliant test. If I succeeded in tolerating the water, I would prevent something bad from happening. I wasn't sure what that thing was, but I could feel it in my gut, as surely as I knew Mom loved me.

I shook my head clear and looked down into the bath. The tub's taunting escalated until I could stand it no more. I plunged one foot into the water, the pain ascended from my foot and spread up my calf. I stood one-legged, like a heron, my free leg pulled into my chest, terrified to enter the watery hell below.

After the initial burn and the responding elation at my power, I looked down, noticing the precise line on my skin at the surface of the water, where my white flesh became red, like a barber's pole, one color dependent on the other for its hue, as if the submerged skin sucked out any possible color from the leg above.

I smiled as I realized the throbbing was actually manageable. I hadn't jumped out. I hadn't cried. I narrowed my eyes to every detail, as if I were looking down from above, floating on the ceiling, observing a stranger's leg. I marveled how the nails of my submerged foot were almost beautiful—a small string of rubies.

But I wasn't finished. I needed to submerge my whole body to pass the test. The pressure in my head rose to a hum, muffling the pain. Come on, you worthless coward—finish the job.

I dropped into the water, my teeth clenched, locking out any shriek that might escape. The agony shot into every orifice of my skin, throbbing, tightening—threatening to burst open, like Dad's tomatoes.

CHAPTER TEN

Dad often left for a week or two, with no communication with any of us about when he'd return. He'd just climb in his truck and we wouldn't know if he'd be gone ten minutes or ten days. One good thing about his absence was my compulsion to tap the doorframe or take scalding baths lessened. In truth it wasn't just me who was different. We all were relieved, relishing in his absence and our freedom.

His return would be just as sudden, and always caused my stomach to cramp, for I never knew when it might happen. It might occur as KK and I giggled with friends spending the night, or early in the morning when he'd pound on the bedroom door and announce he needed us for a chore.

One day when I was thirteen one such return made my breath catch as Dad's truck passed right by KK and me on our walk home from a friend's house. I tried to conjure up an imagined other father, one who pulled over to ask if we wanted a lift—or greeted his kids and asked about their day.

I held my breath and tapped the doorframe three times before I entered the house.

Throughout the afternoon I'd stare through the big kitchen window that looked out into the orchard, expecting

Dad to appear, but other than his red truck looming on the pavement, there was no sign of his return from the Sierras. No whistling as he moved through the trees, lifting a hand to stare closely at a leaf or branch; no boots scraping on the threshold announcing his arrival to make dinner; no three-hour dinner lecture about modern astronomy. But I felt his presence as certainly if he were right here in the room with me. That was the thing about Dad. He was everywhere.

Toward evening, as I was doing homework, Mom left for a school board meeting. I was watching a huge cumulous cloud fade to grey when there was movement under the avocado tree, now deep in shadow. Dad rose off his napping cot and stumbled to his office. Had he been there all along? The light switched on, the door closed.

Although his office was still off limits to me, I didn't care. When he left for the mountains I continued to sneak inside that room, taking it all in, as if I missed him: the hypnotic smell of cigar smoke that clung to the wood-paneled walls; the roll-top desk with its blueprints and dozens of locked compartments; the spare roll-away bed with the Indian blanket splayed across it. I wanted an office just like it. A place away from the house to retreat to, a just-for-me place to write and dream and read. A place free of quirky tapping and scalding skin.

The next day KK and I woke up to the sound of tapping on our bedroom window. "Got a job for you two. Five-minute warning."

We scrambled to our feet and threw our clothes on.

"But I'm hungry," KK said as we walked through the kitchen to get to the back door.

I cuffed one of Dad's bear claw pastries off the counter and tore it two, handing her half of the gooey blob. "C'mon let's go." I pulled on her sleeve. The screen door slammed and we headed to the back of the property. I tried to ignore the sense of loss I felt now that Dad was back home. Normally KK and I spent several days after his return reminding each other of our freedom of just a few days earlier when we could invite friends over to play. I didn't mention how I hadn't boiled a pot of water for a bath in a week. I was trying to keep all of that a secret.

As KK and I emerged from the back door in search of Dad, a sense of playfulness tugged at me, an unwillingness to relinquish the joy I had felt in Dad's absence. I hooked my arm into KK's and began to sing a Beatles' hit from the movie *"Help!"*

"For I have got. . . another girl," I sang, conjuring up the memory of Paul McCartney's hand strumming a girl as if she were a guitar. Oh, how I wanted to be that girl! I gyrated around and pulled KK into a dance while I sang. She laughed and tried to follow, but somehow our legs got tangled and she fell out of my arms.

I spun to catch her, my arms grabbing the air, missing her body completely. She dropped onto the pavement, and although I tried to help her, she rolled away from me sobbing, cupping her left knee with her palms.

How had I messed up so completely? Why couldn't I have just walked out the door like any normal person? I remember thinking I could fix this. I could help her hobble back to the house, maybe even carry her inside. But then what? Mom was off singing as usual, and we didn't have bandages or medicine in the house.

I knew Dad would know what to do, like he had when Mom fell from her horse. I gulped at the memory, and looked up to see he was already running toward us—his legs fluid, like a wild cat, his face just as dangerous, red and tight jawed.

"I am sorry. . . " I put my hand on the ankle of KK's hurt leg and I looked down through her fingers to see blood oozing onto the knee of her jeans.

"Get away from her," Dad said as he swooped KK into his arms like a medic in a battle scene. I tried to follow as he marched to the house, but he spun around, his eyes narrow slits. "Go to your room. I'll deal with you later."

An hour later Dad opened the bedroom door. My words flew at him, grateful to be heard. "It was an accident. Our feet just got jumbled up." Dad shot his hand out, the universal stop sign. I cringed. "But Dad, I didn't mean to hurt her." My voice was too soft.

Dad shook his head. "Pull your pants down."

"I'm thirteen!" My words were loud in my ears.

"Either you pull them down, or I will." I could taste bile in my mouth.

I wept soundlessly as I sat on the bed in my underpants, hoping he'd change his mind. He moved closer, his right hand now on his belt buckle.

His rough hands threaded the wide leather through the buckle, and it hung there while he spoke. "They say this is supposed to hurt me more than it does you, but don't you believe it."

"Please. . . " There was more I had to say, but my throat seized. I began to spiral inward, closing out the world. It was as if I were floating above us both, watching Dad pull on his belt, making it snake out of his pants.

"You've got to learn not to hurt people who are weaker than you." He grabbed the belt buckle end and wrapped it twice around his right palm, flexing his hand each time to adjust the grip. "Bend over."

A hurricane of confusion followed, spinning, spinning, as I watched myself fall to the carpet, squirming to hide my bottom against the side of the bed. "Please, Dad—"

He reached down and grabbed my arm, lifting and flipping me onto the bed in one move. The surprise of it made my breath catch. It made me join my body. A trickle of pee trailed down my legs onto the flowered bedspread. Oh, please don't let him smell it. What would he do to me then?

My head went blank, as if I'd climbed into a black cave. I heard a whistle-hum.

Thwak! He did it. The sting of the belt amplified everything: the squeak of the buckle in his palm; the smack of leather as it hit my skin; the grip of bedspread in my fist.

I heard birds chattering outside my window, and I thought about the Cinderella story—not the cleaned up modern version, but the original, where the birds swoop in and peck out the eyes of each stepsister for being so mean. I imagined the birds in the camellia bush bursting through the window of my bedroom and swarming my father. When they were finished, they would have eaten everything. Even his boots.

But my wishes didn't help. Nobody was going to stop him. That was up to me now. Why didn't I shout or at the very least, get up and run?

———

After that I avoided Dad, and I was grateful for the days he didn't want us around. If we were in the Sierras, this included being dumped off at Pine Acres, an old resort with a swimming pool and cabins for vacationers, nestled in the gold rush county. I was in love with the freedom that Pine Acres offered and was excited whenever Mom dropped us off in heat of the summer. I breathed in the scent of warm pines, red earth, and chlorine, smiling at my luck.

Long before my parents bought the ranch, when Dad first began his love affair with the Sierras, we had spent the summer of 1962 here in cabin #5. I was eight, the summer before third grade, and I thought I was in heaven. The trees, the red earth, and the mountain misery flooded my senses day and night. I could still hear Brenda Lee singing "I'm Sorry" as I leaned back on the porch railing of the cabin and stared out at the trees, a sunburn prickling my skin.

The jukebox was located in Sugar Pine Hall, a huge log room intended as a dance floor, with a set of speakers under its eaves, serenading the trees. Although my rock-n-roll brother Walt would roll his eyes whenever the theme song to *A Summer Place* waltzed into the air, I secretly relished all the tunes in that juke box, a goldmine of melodies-gone-by that formed the backdrop of my life. But my favorite thing was when Nat King Cole's voice crooned "Mona Lisa." The sound would cover the hills like a balm, reminding me of rare moments when Dad would pause and lift his head to sing along.

Fortunately, the property my parents bought was just a few miles from Pine Acres, and it became routine to drop us off there several times a week during summer vacations. We were there so often we even had a tab at the food counter.

On Pine Acres days Mom would pull up to the entrance and we'd pile out before she actually came to a stop. "You two have lots of fun today!" She'd wave her hand and her gold and plastic Bakelite bracelets would clank together.

Frank, the manager would always greet us. He was a dead-ringer for Abraham Lincoln, and he did everything around there: flipped burgers, saved little kids from drowning, and swept up at the end of the day. His kids were awfully lucky to have a dad like that.

Once, the summer after I turned thirteen, KK and I were returning to the ranch from a day at Pine Acres. It was hot, and my thighs stuck to the upholstery. As we drove along, Mom told us our big sister Margery would be joining us for dinner. Margery was twenty-two now and married. It seemed every time I turned around she was telling Mom about ways to get KK and me to lose weight.

"Oh, piffle!" Mom would say, "I was big too when I was their age. They'll grow out of it. You'll see."

But the next time we saw her, she suggested Mom handing us each a can of Metrical for our school lunches this coming school year. I was starving from all the fun we had at Pine Acres, but now I was nervous. As we climbed the driveway I tried to forget about it, and rolled the car window down, the smell of mountain misery and red earth making me smile.

"Dinner in five!" Dad announced as we parked. We dashed inside wriggling out of our swimsuits, laughing about our day and the urgency to help with carrying food to the dinner table. "Two minutes!" Dad called out we walked to the picnic table on the back lawn, where Margery and Dad were already seated at the wooden picnic table.

Dad was stabbing one steak onto each plate. Margery liked her steak rare, and as Dad passed it over, the meat sat like an island in a sea of bloody juice as she carved a bite off. The thought of my heifer leaped into my head. Dad handed me my steak and I fanned the two yellow jackets that escorted it.

Dad frowned. "Don't swat at them, just ignore them. If you get stung, they'll mark you for the enemy, and others will come to attack you. . . and us." Dad speared KK's small steak onto her plate.

I dropped my hands by my side. "Mark me?"

Dad nodded slowly. "Yep, mark you for the enemy. That's how yellow jackets get rid of creatures that pose a threat. They insert a tiny bit of a chemical under your skin, and it serves as a message for the others to dive-bomb you." Dad dropped the subject as quickly as he had started it, sitting down heavily in his chair at the head of the table, his eyes distantly surveying the valley below, like a king.

"Actually, they're just getting meat for their babies." Margery corrected. "Yellow jackets prefer sticky sweet things, like jam." Margery finger-combed her hair behind her ears. Margery liked facts.

The screen door of the ranch house slammed. "Oh, I am so glad you invited me to this party!" Mom announced, carrying a handful of napkins. She sat at the end of my bench.

"This looks so scrumpdiddly-uptious!" I smiled at the change of topic as Dad cleared his throat.

He pulled a piece of paper out of his pocket and unfolded it. "I have a tab here for this month's food at Pine Acres. It's rather surprising. I'd like a real accounting of what you two eat there each day."

I clenched my teeth and looked over at KK, but she was looking down at her plate. Were we in trouble? "There aren't a lot of choices, so we usually have a burger and chips," I offered.

Margery jumped in. "Fat city! Great choice, you guys, especially since I bet you have Cokes and ice cream bars later on, and God knows what else." Was it my imagination, or did she say "Cokes" with an accent. . . like she'd just returned from England? I squirmed on the picnic bench as she dug in deeper. "Do you two even know how many calories are in all that junk?" She carved at her steak.

Dad watched me carefully as he chewed, pausing with his fork in the air to speak. "I'm serious. I'd like a complete account of everything you spent money on today, from arrival to departure. Food, jukebox, everything." His eyes narrowed.

I closed my eyes, trying to remember everything. I began listing it all: quarters for the juke box, burgers, Cokes, popsicles—and late in the day a 50/50 bar each as we waiting for Mom to pick us up. Why did I feel guilty when telling the truth? Had I forgotten something?

"Bah. You know that's not everything! You didn't say anything about candy bars, and I know you had a Baby Ruth or Almond Joy sometime today. What else are you hiding?" He pushed his chair back and folded his arms.

My head spun. We hadn't had any candy. Should I lie and say we had? Would he stop if I did? Dad's stare was focused, like a cobra's. No one moved. We were as silent as an old scrapbook photo. My face was hot. I felt tears on my cheek.

Dad cleared his throat. "Stop the blubbering. Just give me the truth." This was so silly! But he wouldn't give up. Why was he doing this? He was methodically pushing me down, covering me up, demonstrating for the whole family that I was a liar, unworthy of being trusted. I swiped at my wet cheeks and looked over at Margery. Her face had transformed to worry as she chewed her lip. She didn't know the half of what had gone on since she left home.

Mom reached over and touched my hand. "Honey, this isn't a big deal. Just tell your father the truth."

"I am!" I buried my face in my hands.

Mom leaned toward me. "Oh honey, we love you." She patted my hand.

Dad bent his head and lit a Viceroy, staring at Mom. "Speak for yourself." The smoke came out long and slow, hovering above his head like a storm cloud. I looked over at him. What did that mean?

"Pardon?" Mom said softly as if we were at some fancy restaurant.

"I am afraid it just isn't that simple. Love is a tall order. You don't just squander it. Especially without respect."

I looked into his face. "But Dad, I do respect you."

Dad pierced a red cube of watermelon and stabbed it in my direction. "Ah, but the point is, I don't respect you. And since I don't respect you, I cannot possibly love you." My eyes fluttered as I struggled to understand his words.

As if I hadn't heard, he leaned toward me and said it again. "I-don't-love-you." I thought the pause between each word would kill me. The anticipation. The hatred. The truth. My world spun. I gripped the table, my chin quivering. But he wasn't finished. "Try hard to gain my respect, and then we'll see." I held my breath waiting for Mom to say something.

Her eyes darkened as she turned toward Dad, a movement that made my heart leap. Finally! "Oh, Mack." Mom pursed her lips and thrust out her chin. Wasn't she going to say more? But her eyes closed as she bent her head toward her plate, pressing her lips together, sealing in the words. Was she praying?

In that moment, I lost my mooring. I floundered, tossed on the waves of a dark sea, with the realization that the one person I trusted most didn't care enough to throw me a life preserver. At least I knew where I stood with Dad. Mom only pretended to protect me. The silence at the table was unbearable. I crumpled forward, tears flowing over my cheeks and nose, falling onto my legs. My breath came shallow and fast, unable to fill my lungs. Still no words of comfort. With all of their eyes upon me, I moved to the end of the bench, shrinking into as little a space as possible.

There came the sound of a chainsaw somewhere on the mountain. At least it was something, a sound to carry me away from here. When it stopped, I knew I was waiting for nothing. There would be no outrage. No argument. No well-timed rebuttal to bring my father to his knees. I got up and ran fast and hard into the forest, through the clinging mountain misery and pinecones, finally collapsing at the base of a pine tree. Then the truth hit me like a gut punch. Ever since Dad had fallen in love with the Sierras, he had become a thief, each day stealing into our lives and taking something of value. Today it was love. What would it be tomorrow?

For everyone else at that table, life went on as normal. Brownie, our retriever begged for scraps, dishes were cleared, Dad laughed at Johnny Carson as I lay on my bunk bed. Not one family member ever spoke to me about what had happened that evening. It was as if it had never happened.

There were times when I wondered if I had made it all up. Had I been mistaken? Is that why nobody tried to console me? But the memory would return throughout my life with such clarity: The yellow jackets; my shaky voice as I recited the accounting; Dad's words; the silence. It was real. It happened.

Time and again I would bring it up to Mom, asking why nobody said anything, but she had a talent for silencing certain topics, preferring to discuss only the positive. She'd mask the tension we all lived with by suggesting lavish weekends in San Francisco, or shopping trips and dining out whenever Dad left for the Sierras.

A year later when I was fourteen, as Mom drove me to a ballet rehearsal, I took a final stab at asking her about what happened that day in the mountains. I had to know. I was tired of pretending things were okay.

"Why did Dad say he didn't love me?" I watched her face closely. She looked tired, as if she had been expecting my question.

"He didn't really mean that, honey." Mom was looking over her left shoulder to merge onto the freeway. Her words felt like a curtain covering the truth. "God's your real parent, anyway. You need to remember that you're God's perfect child. He loves you just as you are."

Just as I am? Did that mean there was something wrong with me? I closed my eyes. I certainly didn't feel perfect. I was ugly and unlovable. And what did being God's perfect child have to do with Dad saying he didn't love me? It felt like Mom was trying to silence me.

I moved as far away from her as possible, my cheek pressed against the passenger window, cool on my hot face. Looking out at the fading sky, the world rushed past, a swirling mass of grays, where sky met freeway.

Mom began to breath-whistle a nameless tune, her signature sound when bothered by something, something she needed to "see through" and transform into a happy thought. I wanted to vomit as a certainty about my life gripped my chest, making it hard to breathe. I knew then that there would be no help, not from her or anyone else. I was on my own.

CHAPTER ELEVEN

Mom was gone a lot too, mostly to San Francisco, fostering her love of theater and opera. When we were younger, Mom was uncomfortable leaving us in the care of Dad in the evenings ever since she found out he'd drive off as soon as she left. But as I got older and capable of handling things, she left as often as she could. Since Dad had sworn off joining her long ago, sometimes she took us along, but mostly often she invited friends, especially if they'd drive.

One night in the late summer of 1969, when I was fifteen, Mom waltzed out the door in satin and pearls and I heard Dad's truck rev up and drive off not ten minutes later. It was no big deal. I actually preferred it that way. KK and I stayed up late watching TV and listening to the Mamas and Papas, and I fell asleep in her bedroom since we were the only ones home and my parents never let us lock the doors.

We were fast asleep hours later, when the sound of tires on the driveway snuck into my dream, and I froze. Headlights turned the bedroom into a moving stage, scanning across the blue wallpaper. They targeted my record player and a stack of forty-fives, the old Barbies and the herd of Breyer horses. They hit the bookshelf and I saw the pastel spines of KK's Winnie the Pooh collection and our Nancy Drews neatly lined up in order.

As far as I could tell, we were alone in the house. I slipped out of bed, my footfalls soft on the carpet. I peeked out of the bedroom window, but the car hadn't yet arrived at the curve of the driveway, where most visitors parked. It was from this very same window that I had watched Margery neck with boyfriends at the end of her dates.

I needed to find out if we were alone. I crept to my parents' bedroom. Empty. I returned to KK's bedroom and flattened my body against the wall to the left of the window, knowing that because the bedroom window stood at the front of the house, if I were to stand in front of it, whoever was outside could see me. I was grateful for the abundant camellia bush just outside, which partially hid the window but gave me a great vantage point. Suddenly a police car was framed in the window.

"What is it?" came KK's voice, thick and sleepy. She turned her head away from the light, and hugged the comforter.

I whispered, "Nothing. Go back to sleep."

I sank to the carpet and waited for KK to fall back to sleep. The moon offered a pool of light beneath the window, soft and magical. I wanted to stand in it, but I hugged my knees to my chest and took stock. It was almost 1:00 a.m. Who could be in that police car other that Dad? It wouldn't be the first time he was driven home. I heard KK's dreamy breaths, like a slow, pillowed metronome, and got up.

The police car idled like a panther at the curve that led to the steps to our front door, not fifteen feet from where I stood. If I squinted, I saw everything. The moment the headlights were extinguished, the car was swallowed by black. I wanted to wake KK up and tell her all about it but I quickly changed my mind. I needed silence. I needed to figure out what to do.

No movement came from inside the car, but moonlight reflected off the police car's roof—so peaceful sitting there in the dark, no trace of urgency or tragic happenings. Two shapes moved slowly inside the car. Was one Dad? As the hulk in the back moved, the moonlight spread over his head, and the sight of the baby-fine blond hair stopped my breath. Dad. His hand sloppily gesticulated, and I imagined him telling a grand story to the officer, explaining that he wasn't actually drunk, that he had fallen asleep and was simply disoriented. This had been his story of choice over the years, even when he totaled his truck up in the sierras, and he had to sleep in the jail for a night. In each case the details changed slightly, but his message was always the same: I'm not drunk, just sleepy.

A young officer got out, brown hair slicked back, in a neatly pressed uniform. He opened the back door. He bent his body into the back seat and emerged with both arms wrapped around my unkempt father. The officer struggled to support Dad's slack body, rotating himself so only one arm was wrapped around my father's waist.

As he rose, Dad wobbled in his boots, his gangly legs uncooperative, and his arms flopped over the shoulders of the officer's crisp uniform. Being this close, I saw and heard everything. Dad and his voice came out thick as he continued the charm, speaking loudly into the officer's ear. "What are the Giants' chances this year?"

The officer was concentrating on his task, and didn't answer. I remember his face in the moonlight, my eyes followed his every move. With two upward jerks he pulled my father into walking position, and they slowly climbed the wide terra cotta steps to the front door of the house. Dad was unable to straighten his legs or keep his head looking forward. His mouth was turned toward the officer's, and he continued his attempt to wear down the officer, to get him to talk.

Finally the officer spoke. "Not much farther to your door, sir."

I could hear the officer's exhaustion. I wanted to yell out the window that I was sorry. I recoiled at the sight of Dad's weakness, and joined the officer in the sensation of shouldering a misshapen but all too familiar burden.

I don't recall leaving the bedroom or deciding to go to the front door, but I arrived there just the same. Frozen to a spot of beige carpet, I wished I were someone else's daughter. I stared at the door and listened to the sounds Dad made as he leaned heavily against the outside of it, his hands making muffled scrapes on the wood as he attempted to keep himself upright. The officer leaned across my father's chest to ring the bell.

"Awww, Jesus. You don't need the bell," Dad slurred.

Oh, please don't let him come in, I prayed. The doorbell rang one more time, and I remember thinking the officer did this to warn us. He was giving us time to prepare. The knob turned.

I caught them both by surprise. The officer's voice rose upward, like a siren when he saw my face. "Well, here we go, sir. This your daughter?" Dad muttered something and stumbled into the room. He shot me one piercing sideway glance as he moved past. The officer didn't catch it, but the familiar look silenced my lips like glue. Even incoherent and stumbling, he had power. Dad pitched forward and caught himself, leaning his right shoulder hard against the wall, his back to the door.

With eyes downcast, the officer lifted his hand, a gesture I took to be a wave. He backed out of the doorway. "You can collect your truck tomorrow. Have a good evening, now." I didn't close the door after him. My eyes followed him to his car, and out onto the road. I wished that I were in that car with him, driving away. I wished it more than anything. Then I turned to face my father.

Maybe it was the cool night air, or perhaps it was my burning outrage, or the searing contrast between my father and my friends' dads. As I look back now, I see that everything that had gone on before brought me to this one perfect moment, when I had to do something to save myself. My voice came out louder with each carefully chosen word. "Why do you do this? You have. . . a problem. Dad, you can't even walk."

My father rolled his body so that his back was propped up against the wall, his crimson face round and looming, like a harvest moon. He spoke softly then, almost kindly, each word a candy-coated bit of poison for my ears. "I was too sleepy to drive. That's all. If you can't see that, then you're the one with the problem. In fact, you are the problem."

I stood silent as the words came toward me. They hurt, but it was the pain of desperation and sadness. The frustration of things left unsaid. His words skimmed over my body, pressing into me before burying themselves in the carpet beneath my feet. I shook my head and walked to my bedroom grateful for the anchor of my sister's soft snores. As I replayed the evening in my head, my body softened. I felt the weight of it on the mattress.

I didn't kid myself that this was the last time I'd have to confront my drunken father, or shield myself from the terror of his words, but tonight I felt an opening of something new. I had faced him, spoken the truth, and survived. I felt light, as if still floating in my dream. I turned my face to the gibbous moon suspended just outside the window, and smiled at her beauty. I whispered to her, "I am not the problem."

—————

A few weeks later when my sophomore year began at Saratoga High I really felt the loss of my brothers. Walt was in Canada, avoiding the draft, and Don had left for Vietnam. I was struck by the emptiness their absence created. No more laughing in their bedroom; no more jam sessions with friends in the living room. Now it was just KK and me to absorb whatever happened.

In the last year both KK and I had been having difficulty reading the blackboard at school. One evening in early fall, as Dad was reminding us that the upcoming weekend he'd need us for chores, KK blurted out, "Dad, I need to see an eye doctor. It's affecting my grades." Dad looked over as he spun his spaghetti into his spoon. I snuck a look at Mom. She pursed her lips. She'd known about this for months.

Dad frowned and reached for the saltshaker.

"Dad, this is important. My Spanish teacher asked me to translate a sentence on a flash card he was holding, and I couldn't even see it. I squinted hard, which used to sort of work, but I couldn't."

A corner of dad's lips retreated into his cheek, a distorted half smile, as he speared a tomato. "Vision loss doesn't happen overnight. You probably just didn't study."

"No! This has been going on for a long time. I was getting an A in Spanish. Senor Burns has always relied on me to get the right answer. But today I had to say, 'No se, Senor Burns. . . and everybody turned and stared, like I was a dope." KK's face crumpled. "I'm not lying. I really can't see!"

Dad put his fork down and turned toward her. I thought about how the same thing had been happening to me ever since junior high began, but because of Mom, I never mentioned it. I certainly never imagined bringing it up at the dinner table. That would mean having to endure the secret argument that often raged between my parents, one that was felt but not heard. Our dinners were bad enough without adding that.

Once, in sixth grade, the school nurse came to show all the girls a special movie and Mom had given me an official note on Christian Science Mother Church letterhead, all the way from Boston, excusing me from the talk. But I never handed it in. I stayed right in my seat as the lights dimmed and the black-and-white ovaries and vagina appeared on the screen, and I learned about the mysterious secrets of the menstrual cycle. I figured it didn't hurt her not to say anything later, but the whole time I kept thinking about what it was like being Dad, and wondering why Mom would want me to miss the coolest lesson of the year.

The truth was that I'd been squinting for years. I even pretended to be stupid to hide what was really going on because I didn't want anyone to start asking my parents questions. And here KK was opening her mouth, and Dad was all ears.

Dad shot his chair back and stood abruptly, like a missile. "Let's see about that." He walked across to the blackboard on the kitchen door and drew something with the chalk. He tapped the board with a fingernail. "What's this say?" I would have given anything to see what he wrote as I craned my neck forward. But even with my best squinting, I couldn't.

Panic enveloped KK's words. "I don't know."

Dad exhaled loudly and turned his gaze on me. Was I in trouble? Was he going to blame me for KK's vision loss? I tried to shrink into my chair.

"What about you? Can you read it?" He made one loud tap on the chalkboard.

I shook my head no. "It looks like a white smear." I'd chosen my meekest voice. The one that sounded like a question.

Dad squeezed his eyes shut. Was he angry? It didn't matter. I couldn't very well lie since I had no idea what he had written on the board. Dad looked over the rim of his reading glasses at Mom. Up until now, she hadn't said a word. She never interrupted him when he got like this.

"Tomorrow your mother will make an appointment for

you girls with my eye doctor." Mom's breath caught, but she said nothing. Was she really going to dial a doctor's office? Take us to the eye doctor? I couldn't believe my luck. It wouldn't be long before I'd be taking my driving test and I'd been worrying about whether or not I'd be able to read the signs. From an early age Dad had me drive the old army jeep, and I knew I was a good driver in the hills, even though I had to squint, but the city was different. Now I could almost feel the wind in my hair as I rolled down the windows and sped down the highway.

It seemed so simple, and all because of my baby sister's declaration. If it hadn't been for her, Dad never would have known. I'd never said a word. I'd chosen to do poorly in school because I couldn't see. I'd cringed through life, giving an Oscar performance that everything was normal, while keeping quiet, like someone's hand had slipped over my mouth. I was a coward, just like Dad had said.

A week later, I held the door open for Mom and KK, standing in the borderland between the heat of the pavement and the sub-zero cave of the optometrist's office. The air-conditioned chill blew across my skin. Jesus, turn that thing off.

I had no idea what to expect by coming here. Would Dad's doctor really help me? I rubbed my bare arms. A drooping plastic Ficus tree stood in one corner, each leaf a replica of its neighbor, its artificial sheen dulled by dust. What was it about adults who preferred fake over real? If you have to buy one, at least have the decency to clean the poor thing occasionally. How awful to be stuck in the corner, forgotten like that.

Mom took a seat in the corner, crossed her legs, and pulled the *Christian Science Monitor* from her purse, snapping it open on her knee. I wished Mom could just for once be like every other mother and not draw attention to herself. If Dad had brought us here, we'd fit in. This was his doctor, he'd be chatty with the receptionist and make her smile. But that's not how it happened. He never drove us anywhere. Besides, he insisted that Mom do this. No wonder she was tense.

Mom's newspaper was worn, like she'd already read it cover to cover. I looked back at her as my name was called and I was escorted from the room. She didn't look up, just chuckled at something in the paper, her laughter a weapon against this alien world. If I didn't know better, Mom seemed to be enjoying herself. Like she was sitting on her bed on a lazy afternoon. I wanted to call out her name, like I did when I was little. But I couldn't. How uncool would that be? I was fifteen, for Christ's sake.

The doctor beckoned me from the hallway, the bulk of her body curtained by her stiff lab coat. I tapped the door-frame three times and entered.

"You can stand right there." White Coat didn't even look up from her clipboard. "How long has it been since your last eye exam?"

It was as if she were interrogating her clipboard, pen poised, ready for a response. The way she said it transformed the simple question into an accusation. Did she think it was my fault I had never been to an eye doctor before? I shoved my hands into my bellbottom pockets, and felt the sharp curve of my hips.

White Coat massaged her temples. "Did you hear me?" I hated this woman and I had only been here a minute. I pressed my back against the wall as I stood facing her, and held my breath seven seconds before responding. Two steps back and I could easily flee. But then I imagined the freedom of a driver's license tucked into my wallet as I sped down the road heading for the hills.

Suddenly I was aware of a staccato beat, like a fingernail

tapping on a blackboard. I looked up and White Coat was still waiting for my response, her pen poking the paper in front of her. "Do you remember? Now is not the time to be shy. I need to know the history of your eye care." Eye care? If I admitted the truth, wouldn't Mom get in trouble?

White Coat exhaled a breath of air and marched to the end of the short hallway and picked up a pointer, touching it to the long eye chart on the wall. "What's the first line you can see?"

"It's an E. . . I think."

White Coat's chin pulled into her neck. "You think?" I wanted to kick her. She reminded me of my fourth-grade teacher, Ol' Fireball, the one who rolled her eyes and dragged my desk to the back row for 'not trying'. I couldn't see that writing either.

How could I tell her that when I was little I didn't even know there were things on the blackboard that others could see? And once I'd figured it out, I couldn't mention it. It was impossible to explain to someone raised outside of Christian Science how the religion took hold. How it molded me in every way, made me silent and careful. Were there even words to describe this thing we didn't discuss? It was easier to pretend to be stupid.

CHAPTER TWELVE

When I was seventeen, Dad granted my wish and let me borrow his truck so I could make it to ballet class. He leaned against the driver's side door of the Chevy and dropped the keys into my palm. "I'm only doing this so you can rush home after class to get dinner on the table. Don't get used to it. The *Joy of Cooking* is on the table and you'll find recipes for everything you'll serve this evening—tomato sauce from scratch, using the tomatoes I just picked from the garden, spaghetti, Caesar salad, and garlic bread. I want it all ready at the same time, so there's some thinking involved. Don't lounge around after dance class gabbing. Understand?"

I pinched my lips together. Just once I wish I could go to ballet and hang out with the others. We'd walk into town and get a Tab. Or maybe we'd gather outside the dance studio and practice. That would never happen, but I felt the keys, cool and metallic, in my hand. Closing my fingers around the ignition key, I felt the serrated edges in the shape of a sword.

I nodded at Dad. It didn't matter what he said. I had the keys now. And was it really so awful that he counted on me to make dinner? I had lots of friends who couldn't even boil an egg, let alone make a Caesar salad. And now Dad trusted me with his truck. Perhaps he'd found out that Mom asked me to drive her places, and that she felt safe with me at the wheel. I suddenly felt confident and lucky and wondered if this was the start of something new.

I made it to the ballet studio in plenty of time to stow the smile and assume the distant demeanor of ballet dancers everywhere. When I stepped onto the dance floor it was as if I had a greater purpose. I was somebody else. Years of concentration, pain, and heartbreak transformed my body into fluid grace as I found harmony in a discordant world. The late afternoon sun cast a golden ribbon onto the floor, and this in turn reflected off the wall of mirrors. As others filed into the room I put my hand on the ballet barre, claiming my place. I felt taller, lighter, confident.

Halfway through class the stately ballet master stopped in his rounds to correct our positions, and he turned his face to speak to me, looking down his bird-of-prey nose. He offered a rare smile and asked why I didn't always dance like this for him. I paused in my arabesque. I chose not to break my pose, but in my heart it was Christmas morning and I was leaping around the room. I slowly extended my arm and leg in opposite directions, in perfect form. He nodded and moved on to the blonde in front of me.

My body was drenched in sweat when I climbed up onto the truck's running board and collapsed into the Chevy's bench seat. I started the ignition and began the four-mile drive home. As I climbed the hill the truck felt stiff. My brows pressed together as I nervously checked the rear-view mirror. Smoke mushroomed from the tailgate, following me up the hill. I knew I should pull over.

But then I remembered a conversation I'd had with my driving instructor. I'd been fifteen and a half in the fall of 1969, and as we drove along a country road covered in yellow leaves my teacher brought up the latest letter from the

Zodiak killer that had just been published in the *San Francisco Chronicle*. "If anything goes wrong with your vehicle, do not get out of your car or hitch a ride. Ever. Not these days, anyway. I don't want to hear your name on the list of people he's killed."

I'd glanced sideways at the instructor's profile, wishing he'd stop talking about this.

"Sorry," he said. "I never thought I'd have to include that in my lessons, but we're living in a crazy, crazy world."

The Zodiak killer still hadn't been caught, and the fear of being stranded on the side of the road swept through my body. This was picture perfect for him: atmospheric shade trees, a lone vehicle on the road, a stranded teenager walking alone. I held my breath and depressed the accelerator. Home was just a mile away.

By the time I pulled into our long driveway the smoke had turned black. Jesus. I'd made it worse. I parked and jumped from the cab, my sweaty pink tights catching on the woven fabric of the bench seat as I slid to the ground. I looked at my watch and ran to the door. I had two minutes to get in the kitchen before Dad's deadline. I could smell the onions and tomatoes as I opened the back door, and my heart sank. I swore under my breath realizing Dad had jumped the gun again. No doubt he expected me to not follow through with my promise. "Dad?"

He was palming oregano into a pot on the stove as he cocked his head in my direction. He offered the briefest glance and I knew not to question why he'd started my job for me, but the implication that he didn't trust me was clear.

"Dad, something's wrong. There was smoke coming out of the back of the truck as I drove home." I stood in silence, waiting for a response, the sweat from dance class chilling my legs. When none came, I confessed quickly. "I was afraid to stop."

Dad stared into the blood red spaghetti sauce simmering in the ancient cast iron pot, the one that had once been his mother's, the one he said came across the prairie in a covered wagon. I willed him to respond, but it was as if he hadn't even heard me. All I could hear was the agitation of the washing machine in the next room.

My mind raced to make sense of his reaction. Was he deciding how to respond? Had the truck been smoking all week and he forgot to mention it when he handed me the keys? I looked out the window in the silence and almost didn't notice his shaking head. The movement was so small, little wisps of his baby fine hair floating above his head, like dry grass in a puff of wind.

Then he turned at once, looking me full in the face, offering a lopsided grin. But I found his whiskey breath and bloodshot eyes to be too much and my gaze fell downward, where his right fist was opening and closing, like he was squeezing all the juice from an orange.

With my back against the cutting board, I held my breath, waiting for his words to crash down upon me. But he said nothing and thumbed the cast iron pot, as if he were hitchhiking. "Get to work."

He turned toward the door, tossing the red dishtowel on his shoulder onto the counter. His boots scraped the threshold. The screen door hissed open, and smacked closed. I darted to the window where I could watch him discover his truck. A familiar pain tore at my stomach he moved toward the Chevy. Each lift of a leg, slow and uneasy, like he was pushing through oil, no doubt from the whiskey. But when his boots stamped the pavement their power radiated through his body, amplifying his control. Each heel smack of leather on concrete made me cringe.

I went back to cooking the meal, but the longer he was out there, the more my stomach hurt. He had started the truck and it seemed to idle forever. What was he doing out there? What was he going to do to me?

I had just dropped the spaghetti into the boiling water when he entered the kitchen, announcing, "Just as I suspected. You drove home with the parking brake on."

"I did?" I didn't mean to sound challenging.

"Of course you did." He lifted the sauce lid and peered inside. "You can't go around casually destroying other people's things."

I set down the head of lettuce I was bruising. "It was an accident."

Dad frowned, shaking his head, like he was resigned to raising an idiot. "You didn't think it through. I just can't trust you with my truck."

"But how will I get to ballet class and return in time to start dinner?" I tried to mimic his calm, to sound like the good daughter he longed for, but in my head I was grabbing his stupid cast-iron prairie-crossing pot and hitting him hard enough to shut him up.

He slammed *The Joy of Cooking* closed, making me jump. "You *should* have thought about that when you ignored the smoking brakes. You *should* have pulled over instead of racing home—and all because you spent too much time in town with friends."

"No! I came right home after class. I promised you and I did." I was sucking down breaths.

"Bah! Your promise isn't worth a wooden nickel. You damaged my truck."

I stood there shaking, trying to think of a way to explain what really happened. I decided to tell him the truth. I spoke my fears in a rush. "I didn't stop because of the Zodiak killer."

Dad's head pulled back on his leathery neck, putting as

much distance between us as he could without moving his feet. His puffy eyes narrowed like he was aiming his Winchester at me.

"Get off it. Why would the Zodiak killer want *you*?" His nostrils flared when he grated out *you*, as if the word were lodged in the gutter. Then his words melted into a breathy chuckle, as his right hand lifted his handkerchief to his mouth to wipe away the spittle of laughter.

A flush of adrenaline exploded in me like buckshot as I realized what he was saying—that I was so unlovable even a madman wouldn't want me. I stood there listening to the spin cycle of the washer, the insistent revolving of the drum, a soundtrack for my whirling thoughts. I wiped the trickle of sweat that had formed at my temple and bit my lip hard to clear my head.

Dad took another stab at me. "I should have known better than to give the keys to a new driver, and a girl at that."

"You asshole!" shot from my lips, surprising both of us. My eyes went wide, but my body's reaction to the words was pure delicious wonder at the shock of them. No one had ever spoken to Dad like that. It felt like I had burst through a window and soared aloft into the evening air. Nothing could take this freedom from me. Dad stumbled backward. His mouth went slack and a burst of air came from deep inside him. It was as if I had hit him in the gut. Could my words really do that?

"What did you call me?" Dad's breathing reminded me of a bull in the ring. Each word like a hoof pawing the ground. But his body was the opposite, puffed up and sweaty, barely in control. He looked ridiculous.

I realized then that disappointment framed our lives. We each expected more from the other. Neither of us offered what the other wanted. I hated my father, this man whose eyes bulged in surprise at the truth that hung in the air between us.

I narrowed my eyes and reached inside for the ammunition I needed. "You can have your fucking truck. If anyone's a lousy driver, it's you. You're the one who totaled Margery's car and then Mom's, and then came home as if you didn't have a care in the world, claiming you had fallen asleep. Bullshit. The cops didn't believe you. They said you were drunk. How dare you say I can't drive well because I'm a girl. Fuck you!" Inside I was vibrating with power. I had the control now. He was a drunken weakling. A bully on the playground. All bark and no bite.

With one hand on the tile counter he craned his neck forward and reached the other toward me, his red-rimmed eyes meeting mine, still an easy target. I flinched, and then watched in utter fascination as the amber liquid in his veins became the puppet-master, his legs now waving loosely in his boots in an effort to remain standing. I prepared to run, but couldn't tear my eyes from him. His hand shook as it gripped the counter, his body doubling in half, coughing uncontrollably. Or was that laughter?

I wanted to march across the floor and shut him up, but I couldn't bring myself to move in his direction. Had I gone too far? Would he remember this in the morning? I turned on my heel and fled out the front door and down the driveway, certain I'd pay for my words.

"Come back here, god-dammit. I'm still talking to you!" His words came between breaths.

Looking over my shoulder for Dad, but knowing he was too drunk to run, I dodged into the juniper bushes near the roadway, and hid in my best hiding spot—the shadow of that lone pine tree that stood like a sentinel to our property. I sobbed and replayed the scene for what seemed like hours, hugging my knees to my chest.

I later learned that Dad passed out, still in his boots, his body splayed and snoring on the couch. He never found me that evening, but his words did. He didn't need to be there for the barrage to continue. Loud, deformed words stabbed my heart, gaining purchase with each syllable. You're disrespectful. Inferior. Unlovable. *Even a serial killer wouldn't want you.*

Smaller, determined footsteps moved along the driveway.

"You okay?" Relief lit both our faces when KK appeared. She hunched down behind the bushes, out of sight of the house. KK sat with me until the dark came and the words stopped, and the house was a silent crypt.

Sleep that night was an ugly thing. I remember a phone call deep in the night and Dad's truck roaring down the driveway. My thoughts writhed like snakes in a pit, their slick bodies contorting into each other, an ever-changing mass of darkness. Before dawn, I slogged into wakefulness, my head heavy, my eyes so swollen I didn't recognize my face in the mirror. Who was this girl looking back at me? Frozen with fear, I sat down on the bed.

Mom jiggled my door handle, but I had locked it the night before, for fear Dad would barge in. She called from the hallway "Time to get up for school, honey!"

I released the lock, and stared at Mom. "Did Dad go somewhere in the middle of the night?"

She nodded. "He got a call about Sid up at the ranch, and he needed to head up there." I knew there was more to the story. From the crumpled look on her face, this was something big.

"Trouble?" Memories of Sid ran through my head: fishing for dinner together on summer pack trips; his silver hair catching the moonlight as he told stories around the campfire; winking at me as we rode a difficult trail, praising me for my horsemanship; believing me about KK and Mom getting stuck in quicksand, while Dad laughed 'til he cried.

"Sid died, honey. Your father was pretty torn up. He'll be gone awhile."

Dad didn't come back for two months. Mom was the hardest hit by this, but like usual, none of us knew when he'd return. I tried to cheer Mom up when she couldn't hide her sadness, but this leaving was different from the others. It affected us all. This one was mixed with grief over the loss of Sid, and a kind of strange clawing of empathy for Dad I had never felt before. I felt lost and alone, unable to receive comfort. Any relief in Dad's absence was momentary, as week by week the tension grew in anticipation of his return.

But some things changed. My scalding baths gave way to controlling eating behaviors, as if these would give me more control over my life. I lost weight as I dove headlong into dance. I started to craft my escape. I was rarely home, because that's where Dad would go first when he returned.

In late August he walked through the back door with a bag of groceries like he'd just dashed off to the grocery store an hour ago. Oranges were peeking out at the top and I thought back to the orange juice he had made me so long ago, back when I actually believed he could change. I sucked in my breath, my body suddenly tight and tired of everything and everyone. I wanted to shrivel like a leaf and blow away. I wanted to yell and scream at his return. I wanted to hold Mom back from exploding.

CHAPTER THIRTEEN

After Mom swore at Dad for not once calling in all that time, and he'd responded by saying he could do whatever the hell he wanted because this was his home after all; and she'd turned on her heel and fled to the bedroom and he had marched out to his office; and she'd prayed and he'd returned to make her orange juice and then dinner, banging pots and pans, the heady smells of onions and garlic and tomato sauce wafting out of the kitchen, Mom finally forgave him. Or maybe she felt sorry for him, because that's what I was feeling.

He had changed. He had vacant eyes and a fleeting wildness that reminded me of when he had dressed up like an old miner for the Kit Carson parade in Jackson years ago, pulling a donkey loaded with mining gear and burlap sacks—and won first prize.

While I still couldn't invite friends over after school for fear Dad would greet us in his underwear and boots, or worse yet buck naked, the change in him made him less frightening. It almost seemed like he couldn't help it. He demanded less, spending days in his office or on the cot underneath the avocado tree, drinking and reading. At fifty-three, he'd become an old man.

A few weeks later, on Thanksgiving morning, KK and I were preparing the big feast. It felt good to do something normal. Since his return, Dad had given up walking back into the house for anything—even to make meals or use the bathroom.

I stood staring out the kitchen window at him in the orchard. "Did you see what Dad did to his teeth?" His battered cowboy boots blended in with the brown soil and leaves. The soft rays of the November sun barely warmed his threadbare Pendleton shirt and he slapped his hands on his upper arms to get warm. A lone mockingbird called wildly from the chimney and Dad turned to look up at it.

"Yeah, I saw them," KK said, rolling her eyes. She had just turned up Tower of Power on the stereo, and walked back into the kitchen to join me at the window. Music always softened the rough edges of our lives, and we clung to it like a lifesaver. Without uttering a word we were in agreement: Horns and harmony were needed this Thanksgiving morning. The louder, the better.

KK and I were bound forever as best friends, simply by surviving our upbringing. We were strong in entirely different ways, and I tried not to think about her being left behind when I planned to leave in June. But she was smart. . . frighteningly so, and had a way of handling Dad that none of the rest of us could fathom.

We had been appointed the chefs for the day's meal, the first ever that Dad would not supervise, and I was grateful for the freedom. What did we have to worry about? We had each done our two-year kitchen internship with Dad, so we knew how to put together a big holiday feast.

I looked back out at Dad, now fiddling with something in his hands. "Do you think he meant it about not getting dentures?" I asked.

Earlier this week Dad had gone to the dentist for what

we assumed was a routine check-up. When he returned, his teeth were gone. When I asked him about it, he said he told the dentist to take them all out, and had no intention of getting any replacements, dentures, or otherwise. The audacity of his statement shocked me. Yet his unconventional boldness fell solidly into the range of "normal" for a man who would disappear for weeks at a time and then return to haunt our lives in boxer shorts and boots.

Looking back, normal is a ridiculous term to use when referring to my father. Normal when I was a seventeen was me perched on the scrabbly edge of anticipation, holding my breath for his next calculated act. I could only exhale once it was over. I'd have perhaps a day or two while he regrouped and planned, and then the cycle would start all over again. What made this brutal act different was the recipient. He inflicted this on himself. He'd spent a lifetime of not caring for his teeth, and now this. It hit me then that I couldn't remember him holding a toothbrush. What's more, he didn't seem phased by his decision. This twist was more than a little unsettling.

Dad's head was cocked slightly to the right now, as if listening intently to something underground. He moved methodically, elbows bent against his torso. His eyes fixed upon a wire protruding from each hand. His eyes were watery and hopeful.

"Is he water witching again?" I asked.

"Probably," KK said, walking back to the window to follow my gaze. "He told me he misplaced his whisky bottle. I thought he was kidding when he said he was going to dowse for it."

KK and I had been very young when Dad taught us about water-witching, more commonly known as dowsing. He had been enthralled by his Stanford geology professor who once described the technique in class. Ever since then, Dad took frequent opportunities to entertain himself and others by removing a wire coat hanger from the closet and within minutes producing two L-shaped dowsing rods.

Dad had always been a marvel at finding ground water with those wires. There was no scientific explanation for it, but we had watched him countless times show off in front of visitors who had at first laughed at his assertions that it was possible to locate water this way. If you had "the gift" the wires moved toward each other, in front of your body, to form an "X" above the very spot where water was located underground. Their laughter inevitably turned to admiration because over the years the news of his talent spread and he was often called upon to help the local well driller find water in the Sierras.

The squeak of the fridge brought me back to the room. KK was reaching in and pulling out the twenty-four-pound turkey. I joined her, squatting down to retrieve two onions from the bottom drawer. "I'll start Grandma's stuffing."

"You think we can do this?" KK asked standing over the bird in the sink, and yanking out its neck, heart and kidneys.

"We have to, that is unless you want *Mom to do it.*" This last bit I purred and we erupted in laughter at the memory of kitchen dramas that we had endured when she cooked, most of them involving unrecognizable black things emerging from the oven.

Several times throughout that day Dad scraped his boots on the threshold and stood in the doorway to check on our progress. But as the afternoon unfolded and my siblings began to arrive from out of town, he became like an old bear and retreated to the orchard in search of solitude and comfort.

At 4:00 we'd all gathered at the kitchen table for Thanksgiving dinner when Dad appeared at the back door, the daylong shots of whiskey taking its toll on his posture. KK and I had the best view of his entrance, and were glad to see he had changed his clothes. His jeans were clean and he had traded the dirty T-shirt for one noticeably whiter, although it did have a hole at the shoulder. But his boots never changed. They were rough and water-stained, having endured countless adventures. He sat down next to me at the head of the table and opened his mouth, but the words that escaped were unintelligible.

I'd like to think he was thanking us for the meal, but he wasn't really looking at us. The effort seemed to unsettle him, and he opened his mouth wider, as if this were his plan all along. He jutted out his lower jaw, pulling back his lips into a frightening grimace, exposing his empty gums. This frightened our sister Margery's sons, and her youngest, just barely two, began to cry.

Margery recoiled. "What happened to your teeth, Dad?"

"Don't need 'em anymore. Tired of brushing and going to the dentist." The very toothlessness of his garbled confession made us all lean forward to squeeze meaning from his words.

"What?" Margery asked, turning her head quickly and staring at Mom, as if she were at fault. I was sorry Margery had to find out like this. I'd assumed Mom had told her. I looked up at Margery's concern. Recently she had offered to have me move in with her, but now I couldn't leave. I needed to stay and help. Dad went silent and KK and I busied ourselves with passing the huge bowl of mashed potatoes, hoping Margery wouldn't press him further.

Dad seemed more a homeless guest than our father. I stared at him as he attempted to eat. In the end it was the potatoes and gravy that made up most of his meal. He'd scoop some up, closing his mouth over the spoonful and moving his closed lips quickly up and down, the gums attempting to chew. He reminded me of an old sepia photo I'd once seen of a toothless miner.

As dinner progressed, Dad's shoulders leaned closer toward the table, as he mumbled and gesticulated to nobody in particular. No one asked, "Sorry, what did you say?" We were too embarrassed to respond, grateful there were no guests to witness his decline. We simply ignored his mumbling and carried on with our multiple conversations, barely looking in his direction. At some point during the evening Dad lost his power over me.

He just sat, gumming his potatoes and staring at his plate, his silence giving no indication of what was to follow.

Suddenly Dad ducked his head forward, as if avoiding something thrown at him. His left hand grabbed at the air over his plate, reaching wildly for something to hold on to, something he saw but couldn't reach. His hand dropped to the edge of the table, gripping the wood firmly, shoulders hunched over like a mountain. He slapped his right hand on the back of his head. Then, just as suddenly, he flung it out as his head turned sharply to the right. Looking over his shoulder, he punched the air with his finger.

"He's coming! Jesus. . . God. . . No!" He cried as he hunched down in his chair, hugging his knees. The haunted, desperate look in his hazel eyes confirmed my thoughts that he was no longer here with us. Dad was in the chaos of battle, where the unspeakable becomes reality. His imposing body looked more like a frightened child as he caved in upon himself and his memories played out before him.

Every jerk of his body ripped me open, every jarring word a nauseous revelation that I was not the only one wounded at this table. I couldn't offer him anything. I could only witness his pain. I sat still, absorbing all of it. There was a moment when he lay flat, hugging the tabletop. I looked over his head across the table and saw the expectant face of my mother, always so open and radiant, now twisted into a disembodied mask of disbelief.

Our eyes were glued on my father as he writhed at the edge of the table. "Where's Weiler?" he slurred, cocking his head, listening intently to some unheard reply. "Get down! He's coming right at us. Get down. Down! " Then sobs drowned out his words. Mom's face was a movie of emotions, a constantly changing landscape. She caught my glance and I realized she wasn't going to do anything to help. What could she do? Pray?

I began crying next to my father, his big calloused hand shaking on the table in front of me. I thought of reaching out and holding it, but as my hand moved forward I was suddenly seized by fear of his response, and let it fall back into my lap. Would he accept my touch? I had never put my hand in his before. He had never reached out to take mine. The concept was a foreign as a fatherly goodnight kiss. I resorted to words instead.

"Who's coming, Dad?" I asked softly, and then repeated myself in an effort to reach him. "Dad. . . who is coming?"

But he didn't hear me. He was on a destroyer in the Pacific. He was the "Old Man," the lieutenant commander. He was supposed to be calm and prepared, but he wasn't. He was barely twenty-three years old, and the Japanese warplane's angry drone was unbearable as it turned and aimed straight for Dad's ship, carrying just enough fuel to hit its target.

He jerked to the left as if pushed. "We're hit!" He gasped for breath. "Portside! He's in the water—floating portside!" Feeling the weight of his command, Dad attempted to gather himself. "Damage? Casualties? Weiler?"

He must have received a response beyond understanding, for he crumpled, sobbing a sadness so deep he pulled me under with him. His arms covered his head, forehead hard against the table. Fine blonde wisps of his hair mixed with the gravy on the rim of his plate. I looked over Dad's splayed body to my family—KK, Mom, Margery and her little sons, grateful my grandfather wasn't here to see this, horrified the little boys were, the youngest's head buried in Margery's lap.

I looked back down at the table. "Dad?" I moved my head closer to his. He slowly turned his head toward me, opening his mouth to respond, revealing a gaping hole as dark as his sadness.

Three weeks later Dad was taken to the county hospital's alcoholic ward. As I marched across the parking lot in search of the door to the hospital, you would have thought I was angry. But if you had looked closer, you would have seen the fear all over my face. I mean hold-me-tight kind of fear, the kind that wakes you up at night. The kind that makes you cry at kindness.

Don't call me nuts, but I'd hoped Dad would want to see me. All the way to the hospital I imagined he'd reach for my hand and apologize. And yet I knew it wouldn't go like that. I told myself I didn't care if he threw me out. I just had to see him. Most mornings I lie in bed listening to the yellow jackets hover at the open window, wondering why I still love him. After everything he'd done, and said, his words lingering in my head, like a brand.

I stood in front of the hospital receptionist with her bubble hairdo and pearl earrings looking down at my antiwar t-shirt and frayed bell-bottoms.

"I'm here to see my father, Mack Erickson." I sounded like a normal daughter, one who planned to rush to her father's bedside. Was I? Would I? My emotions were like a flammable liquid, stable on the outside, explosive with heat. The receptionist smiled and pointed one manicured finger toward the elevator sign.

The layout of the hospital was incomprehensible. The

corridor turned in on itself like a twisted gut. Everywhere I turned, the hopelessness of weak broth, reconstituted eggs and overcooked peas sickened my senses. I imagined Dad's disgust as he lay in his hospital bed dreaming of curried lamb, homemade spaghetti sauce and watermelon.

I could hear shouting as I emerged onto the second floor hallway. "I'll take that pill if you give me a drink, honey," a voice bargained. I held my breath at the smell on this floor, the mixture of vomit and alcohol growing with each step. I had found the men's alcoholic ward.

The bargainer was still refusing a pill when I reached the doorway and looked inside. His swollen face made it difficult to guess his age. A young nurse was standing beside him with a paper cup. "That's not how this works, Mr. Peters," her voice a no-nonsense form of tenderness.

From the other end of the hallway, a gurney came barreling toward me. The patient on board narrowed his eyes as he approached, and one hand floated up into the air. He limply flicked his wrist. Was he shooing me away? The other hand—more animal than human—pawed the sheet near his head as if he were digging in the sand. The attendant shook his head and pushed the gurney into the room. Did Dad really belong in the same room as this man?

The men's alcoholic ward was a washed-out version of the rooms downstairs, as if the smells and suffering within its walls had somehow sucked out all the color. A fading beige permeated everything except the ceiling, a moonscape with spreading stains in one corner, like spilled coffee. It was a room for the undesirables.

I anchored myself to the doorframe of the detox ward, the pads of my fingertips touching the wood, like a rehearsal. I tapped with both hands three times, but was unable to bring myself to cross the threshold. I looked out at ten men, all in various states of liver damage, shaking, moaning, screaming for relief, and not a single visitor in sight, except for me. I scanned the disheveled patients, looking for my father. Where was he?

My eyes fell on a man whose distended belly rose up like a flesh mountain above the valley of sheets, his belly button protruding, like a fat worm emerging from the earth. It wasn't Dad, but I couldn't tear my eyes away from him. His breathing was shallow and one spindly leg lay exposed, all the way to his crotch, his foot, a mottled purple. My eyes shot to the floor, my face hot.

It was then that I noticed the very last bed in the corner. I leaned toward that familiar shape. It was Dad. His face was turned away from the searing light of the room, his hair matted with dirt and sweat. His legs thrashed separately from his body, like vipers. Just like that, his head snapped toward me, and my body jolted upright, like a soldier.

"Get the goddamned snake off me!" His hand swiped at something unseen in the air. I thought of the rattlesnake he'd shot on that first trail ride we'd taken together in the Sierras, the one bold enough to cross Dad's path. I remember the shattering fear of the blast; the satisfaction on his face as I watched the snake's body twist and turn in the red dirt. My head spun in a firestorm of confusion. Why wasn't anybody helping him? Hell, why wasn't I?

His face turned toward the wall, as if he couldn't bear it any longer. I should do something, but what? I'd expected to feel relief that he was here, finally unable to harm himself or anyone else, but I didn't. I felt guilt. I looked down at my feet, but they refused to move into the room. What the hell was wrong with me?

Suddenly the appalling stench of feces spread through the room, as the man to my right announced, "Get a load of that, boys! The biggest, blackest turd ever!" Someone hooted congratulations, and I turned away, nearly bumping into a large nurse, holding something familiar in her fist. Was that bridle leather?

I fingered the POW bracelet on my wrist, remembering Dad's long ago grip on the leather halter of my frightened heifer, and his reassuring pat on her neck just before he shot her in the head.

At the sight of the nurse, the men in the ward—those who were coherent—fixed their eyes on her hands. I looked back at Dad, somewhat calmer now, his eyes moving back and forth under closed lids. Was he sleeping?

"Joe, let's get you more comfortable," the big nurse said too loudly to the man on the gurney. Her voice reminded me of the old actress Ethel Merman, who spoke like everyone was hard of hearing. She held her brashness like a shield against the misery of the room.

Scary nurse unwound four leather straps, handing two to an attendant. Joe's eyes expanded. They looked like the heifer's. I wiped at my cheek. I needed to do a pirouette *now*.

Joe screamed as they leaned their bodies against him, attaching a leather strap to each hand and foot. They tethered him to the bed frame, while I looked on, as if this were some sadistic play. It happened so fluidly, I wondered how many times each day they did this. Wait. Was Dad tethered too? I looked back at him and saw the brown of leather, peeking out like a memory, next to his head. How had I not noticed the straps before? Of course he was tied down. He was like the poster boy for being a menace to himself and others. So why was my stomach all squirrely?

At the sound of someone retching, I dashed down the corridor to a little alcove with a couch and a couple of chairs. You know the place—where families gather, holding their breath, waiting for anything—even scraps. I curled into a ball, my world inside out. Who was I kidding? I had nothing to hope for. Dad had always been the hurter, not the hurt. But then I remembered his body splayed on the kitchen table at Thanksgiving, his grief unreachable, and I realized I didn't know him at all. What more could I have done?

My head spun. What kind of a daughter was I? Shouldn't I stick around and wait? I imagined being the dutiful child who waited patiently for news. I stuck my hand inside my macramé bag, and grabbed *Walden*, breathing in the perfume of the old book. Just as quickly I shoved it back into my bag, my body heavy with exhaustion.

The truth was, Dad would never want to see me, no matter how long I waited. Nothing was going to change; no love would suddenly blossom when he set his eyes on me. He would never reach a hand out and make all the pain go away.

My face was angry hot. As if I were about to be engulfed in flames, I tore down the sickly green hallway to the stairs, my feet a blur. The big nurse stepped back as I dashed past, her eyes wide. Down, down, down the stairs I flew, as dark thoughts swirled and pooled. I would never be the daughter he wanted. He would never be the father I needed. Nobody would want me. I was unlovable.

CHAPTER FOURTEEN

Dad was back home in no time, having busted himself out of the hospital as soon as he could walk. At first, he seemed to float around the periphery of our lives like a ghost, appearing on the other side of a window or lying in his cot under Susan, the avocado tree in the orchard. I'd look at him through the kitchen window and wonder what he was thinking. Did he know I had shown up at the hospital, but had been unable to come to his side?

None of us ever said anything about his time in detox or asked him about how he was feeling, as if not mentioning these things were kinder. Or maybe a better word is easier. He seemed relieved to be home, but rarely came inside the house, preferring his wood-paneled office that smelled of cigars and whiskey.

Although life was calm, almost surreal, I couldn't help but feel the inevitability of something unexpected popping up out of nowhere. He'd return to detox, or worse. But as the weeks wore on I tried to relax and accept the "new" dad who never ordered us around and seemed muted and ghostly, always on the edges of my thoughts. My battle with him now was internal. A better daughter would have knocked on his office door and asked if he needed anything. Pancakes, perhaps. Or at least a cup of coffee. He had offered me orange juice once, hadn't he? Why couldn't I offer him something in return?

While all of this was happening, Mom was transforming into a different breed of woman, enthralled by her new freedom. Dad was no longer in her way. This was something I hadn't even realized had been difficult for her. She even moved differently, like she had been waiting for this moment all her life. No more a silent caterpillar waiting for what came next. She retreated to her bedroom far less often; she avoided Dad entirely.

It was 1971—and mod orange was everywhere—even on my mother. One day I had come home from school and found her standing there in the living room like a flame-colored butterfly dressed in filmy orange polyester, her gold bracelets clanking together, as she gesticulated. "I've got good news! I'm going to start teaching voice lessons—from right here in our living room."

"Now?" I pivoted to look out the window at Dad. Did he know?

"It's just a few students a week. They'll be gone before you even get home." Her hands fluttered like doves.

I wanted to believe her, to support her idea, but it felt wrong. Things were too weird and new right now. The change we had all gone through was too much, and I wasn't sure I could stand another new thing—let alone strangers coming into our home.

"But what about Dad?" I didn't mean to sound so whiny.

Her hand went to her hip. "He'll just have to get used to it."

I blanched at the new Mom, but inside I smiled. I had no idea this kind of defiance lived inside her. Within a month she had a continual stream of students coming and going. Who knew she'd be so popular? They sang jazz, show tunes, and opera. Some were still in high school dreaming of the spotlight; others were hardworking secretaries or college students or grandparents wanting something more from life. But they all had one thing in common—they loved Mom: Her flamboyance and certainty that they had something inside worth sharing. She was positive and encouraging, always finding the perfect songs to highlight a student's talent. They embraced her encouragement as if they had known all along they were meant to sing.

I can still recall the first time I walked in on a lesson. I had pushed open the front door, and Mom was beaming into the face of her student. I couldn't remember her ever looking at me like that. Her pupil was willow thin and blonde, with a quiet uncertainty that reminded me of the actress in Alfred Hitchcock's movie, *The Birds*.

Mom spotted me in the hallway, her eyes pleading that I not interrupt. She was explaining the warm-up process to her student. "We're going to do some vocalization, dear. Repeat after me: *I yawn!*" My eyes shot wide. Had Dad heard her out in the orchard?

"I yawn," came the student's pensive response.

I nearly giggled at Mom's expression, the wince and quick cover-up as she fought to regain composure. Mom closed her eyes and lied. "Good, dear. Now let's try that again, but this time imagine you are a hippopotamus and you are *very, very* sleepy." At this point Mom tilted her head to one side and mimed falling asleep. Why was Mom talking to this grown woman like she was in kindergarten?

Then Mom quickly straightened up, soldier style, and fixed her eyes on her student. "Now, repeat after me: I yawwwn!" Mom shakespeared the words for the entire neighborhood to hear. Oh man, wasn't our family weird enough?

I thought back to the story Mom used to tell of an audition when she was an aspiring actress in New York City, before World War II. She was nineteen and living with her parents, who supported her operatic vocal training, but never the idea she would dream of ever setting a foot on the stage. My mother had been a debutante and it was her parents' hope that their only daughter would soon be married.

Mom snuck out to auditions anyway. On this occasion, she had been told to memorize the lines of a famous speech. Having very little experience in theater, Mom chose Juliet's balcony scene, the one that begins, "Oh Romeo, Romeo, wherefore art thou, Romeo?"

She snuck out of her parents' apartment and made it just in time for the 9pm audition. She stepped onto the stage and couldn't see anyone in the audience, although she knew the director was out there. Three sentences into her monologue the director's voice boomed, "Miss Johnston. Juliet did *not* hit Romeo over the head with a sledgehammer. Get—off—my—stage!"

Mom would laugh at each retelling of that story, but I knew better. Her chocolate eyes had a twist of pain right in the center. Maybe that's why she wanted to teach so badly, to help others step forward and perform.

I felt like an outsider in my own home, and I slipped down the hallway to my bedroom. Had she even discussed her plans with Dad? Did he even know what was going on? But I soon had my answer.

One afternoon while Mom warmed up a middle-aged lady in a black pantsuit, I heard Dad's boots scrape the back door threshold. I froze, not daring walk into the kitchen where he now stood. Had Mom heard him enter the kitchen?

I ducked down the hallway, out of sight of Dad. Here I had a good view of the living room. I watched as Mom's hands progressed up the keyboard, warming up her student with musical scales, the notes getting higher and higher. Once or twice the student guffawed mid-note at her inability to hit the note Mom played. I instantly liked this woman.

"Everything okay in here?" Dad called out from the kitchen, blinking and running his hand through his hair, like he had just woken up in the kitchen.

At the surprise of hearing his voice, Mom lifted her hands off the piano keys, lips pursed. She reminded me of my school principal. "Mack, I have a student here."

Ah, so she *had* told him about the lessons.

Dad chuckled. "It's just that I came in to retrieve my book and I heard what sounded like an ailing bird."

"Mack!" Mom's voice was foreign and sharp as she jumped stood up from the piano bench and saw him. She faltered slightly, then suddenly stuck her arms out at her sides as she moved in his direction, as if blocking him from going further into the living room. *What was she doing?* I scootched back down the hallway and peered into the kitchen, and saw what Mom saw. Dad was wearing a dirty t-shirt, boxer shorts and cowboy boots. Nothing more. I wanted to crawl out the door and never come back, but I was riveted, watching his every move.

Dad sidestepped Mom and walked further into the living room, toward the student. There followed a painful slow-motion shot of that poor woman registering what Dad was wearing, as she emitted a shock of breath then recovered, closing her eyes and gripping the edge of the piano.

Dad eyed the lady, now just a few paces away from him. "Sorry to bother, but, well, this *is* my living room after all. I'll just be grabbing this." He scooped up Hemmingway's *For Whom the Bell Tolls*, and marched back out the door, winking as he brushed past Mom, a twisted "gotcha" on his face.

I stood transfixed as the student slowly opened her eyes, a look of such compassion on her face, it sealed her commitment to my mother and her lessons for the next decade.

But the weirdness had just begun. The next day when I came home I smelled whiskey in Dad's wake. The ghostly "good" dad was gone. Now he stumbled in and out of the house at will, as we kept silent, never mentioning anything. I hoped Mom would say something about his clothes or the drinking, but she never did. She couldn't. She only saw the good.

Dad's boot steps still had a kind of old-man shuffle, having somehow lost all but a shadow of their angry grip. This change made me sad.

———

A few nights later I was watching a movie on the TV. KK and Mom were attending a concert and Dad had left, even though he wasn't supposed to drive. I had built a fire in the fireplace and I fell asleep on the floor during the Johnny Carson Show. Deep in the belly of the night, something—someone touched my back, a fat finger running from my neck to my bottom. I was up on my feet before I was even fully awake, squinting at a shape of a stranger sitting on our couch, staring at me, his eyes reflecting the glow of the fire's embers. He was wild-haired and tense, like a fox in the wild.

"Aw, don't worry," the man garbled, reaching his hand out again. I could smell the stink of whisky wafting off his skin. I kicked at him and ran down the hallway to Mom's room.

I shook her mattress. "Mom! There's a drunk in our TV room and he's trying to touch me."

From her voice I could tell she hadn't been asleep. She sounded tired. "Let's not call him names, honey. Apparently he came home with your father last night—drove him home, in fact and needed a safe place to sleep, that's all."

"That's not all! I was asleep on the floor—did you know that? He touched me. He scared me!" What was wrong with her? Why wasn't she listening?

Mom patted my back like I was six. "Oh you're imagining all that—he couldn't have known what he was doing."

Her denial made me want to slap her. Why did she always have to only see the good in other people? Couldn't she see I was telling the truth?

After that I stayed away from home as much as possible. Usually that meant I was at my best friend Julie's house down the street. One day, not long after Mom started to teach lessons, Dad was pacing the kitchen floor when KK and I returned from Julie's. I had been gone so much, I felt like a visitor. As I stared into his face I realized I hadn't actually seen him in over two weeks. The change was nauseating: His watery blood-shot eyes; the half a dozen bruises on his yellowing skin all in various stages of healing; his sour smell and matted hair. I felt like hosing him off, like he used to do when we returned from the beach. I forced myself to remember: This is my dad. *My* dad.

Then he spoke. "You two come with me. You're never going to believe what happened while you were gone." KK and I eyed each other. Did we have to?

He crooked a calloused finger, beckoning us to follow. What was it about that small movement that scared me? Was he really so dangerous?

Dad actually looked fairly comical in his clown-like appearance. Even so, every bone in my body warned me not to follow. But it was as if some invisible hand had been cupped over our mouths, and just like that—KK and I got up and followed him out the back door, like a couple of robots. What else could we do?

"Where are you taking us?" KK asked as the screen door slammed behind us.

"To show you the evidence of the intrusion." Dad nodded to himself as if he liked the idea of what he just said, as if he wasn't the one who had just said it. It's funny how this small thing set me off. This small change in him was like neon on our walk. You think you know your dad, and then bingo—he has a new mannerism. It was the newness that scared me, and I didn't like it one bit.

"Intrusion?" KK mouthed, more to me than to Dad.

He turned and opened the door to a detached building that housed two rooms: our pantry with its big chest freezer and the wood-paneled boys' room—where my brothers used to sleep when they still lived here. Now that they had left home it was empty, except for the player piano and two lumpy single beds. The room smelled stale as we passed the pantry. I realized Dad would never make dinner for us again. He marched straight into the boys' room, and walked over to the piano, pointing a finger at the keyboard. "*There's* the evidence of your intruder." He kept nodding like a bobble-head.

KK blurted, "Dad! How did that get there?" I followed her gaze and saw the smears and blobs of blood all along the piano's keys, like someone had slowly dragged a bloody finger down the length of it.

I willed my body to suck in air as I looked into Dad's granite face.

"Isn't it obvious?" Dad said solemnly. "That is the intruder's calling card."

"But Dad. . ." KK whispered. We both knew there had been no intruder. But now what? What kind of a universe had Dad entered? I was suddenly reminded of eleven years earlier when Dad pointed to the hills behind our house describing the Abominable Snowman. Wasn't this just more of the same? Or did he really believe the insanity he was spewing?

The bloody keys made me think of the Zodiak killer who was still out there somewhere. The oppressive "This could happen to you if you're not careful" attitude seemed to be everywhere like a noxious gas. Had the world gone mad?

My eyes searched his hand for some cut on the skin. It could have been so casual, almost an afterthought. How many times had I asked him about a cut on his finger or hand and he'd look down with surprise at the red trickle of blood as it dripped to the ground. How come he didn't feel it? He had to have been the one who bloodied the piano, but why?

Dad's watery eyes lingered on our faces. His next words were almost kind. "I'll need to stick around and make sure he doesn't come back."

The blood on the piano changed everything. After that Dad stumbled in on Mom's lessons whenever he felt like it. It was like he planned it, his boots scraping the threshold, warning of intrusion. He'd burst into the kitchen singing the Toreador aria from the opera Carmen, drowning out the student's voice altogether. Mom would purse her lips and try to ignore his beautiful tenor voice. It was in those moments I realized one thing she must have found attractive so long ago. How could it have gone so wrong?

One day after Dad spiraled out of control, I came back from ballet class and found KK and Mom deep conversation on the other side of Mom's closed bedroom door. "No, Mom! It isn't better to stick around 'til I'm out of school! It's just putting off the inevitable. Don't you get it? You've gotta take us out of here."

KK's passion stunned me. I had not realized she had been harboring these thoughts, let alone that she'd speak to Mom like she had it all figured out—like she was the real parent. I mean, we never ever knew what we'd come home to, but something new must have happened. Some barrier crossed. Or maybe I was just so numb to my life I didn't know what to do or how to save myself.

Within a week Mom began to casually discuss the possibility of divorce with us. The lightness of her decision made me boil inside. She could have left at any time. In all the years that Dad had harmed and humiliated me, never once had she protected me by threatening to divorce him. But now, when his actions got in the way of her image and her business—and the fact that KK brought it up, divorce was all she could talk about.

My head was a jumble of confusion. I didn't want to stay with Dad, hadn't even seen him in several days, and yet I felt like a traitor with Mom's secret inside me.

"I'm going to tell your father this Saturday," Mom said one day after school. What would his reaction be? Would he even notice? "And after that we'll need to discuss what to bring with us when we go. I'm thinking it might be best to leave everything here. Start anew. . . doesn't that sound like fun?"

Fun? This new mom was nuts. "*Everything* stays?" I asked. No couch? No kitchen table and chairs? No beds? And what about all those trolls we had left in the attic? I couldn't remember the last time we had gone up there to play. . . several years, at least. I could just see it, a frozen village of happy trolls with their psychedelic hair and big grins. Shouldn't we at least clean *that* up? But the very idea of quietly climbing up there to the place we'd cleared right above Dad's wood-paneled office, where he was at this very moment taking a nap or worse, made me nauseous. I looked over at Mom. Maybe she was right. I listened to her plan and tried to be hopeful.

"Of course we'll bring the grand piano and my bedroom set," Mom said. It sounded like an afterthought. I understood the piano, which had been in her family for ages. . . but her bedroom set? I thought about the ornate carved maple bedroom set that Dad had given her as a wedding present. What was she thinking? Wouldn't this upset him?

On Saturday morning Mom stood in the doorway to KK's bedroom before "the talk" with Dad in the kitchen—her face determined, looking down at both of us as we pretended to be absorbed by Elton John's latest album, *Madman Across the Water.* I wanted her to just get it over with. She turned and entered the kitchen, closing the door behind her. As much as I resented her, divorcing Dad was my only way out. KK was right. We couldn't stay here.

Would they shout? Would he hurt her? Fuck my homework. I leaned my ear against the door and tried listen, but all I could make out was soft mumbling for what seemed like hours. Then I heard Dad cry and call out her name as the clip-clop of her heels retreated out of the room. After that all I remember is a dark nothing.

Within a month, Mom bought a new condo being built in a nearby town and rented a do-it-yourself moving truck. She encouraged us to put our personalities into our new bedrooms, and over time we got excited about the move. We visited the condo development several times to take measurements and make flooring decisions before our unit was finished. I pushed for hardwood, preferring the cool hard slap of wood under my feet, but I was out-voted. Mom decided on long green shag carpeting because it reminded her of spring. It looked like crazy overgrown grass that somebody needed to mow. Mom produced a carpet rake mentioning that before her students came she'd like it to be raked neatly. She meant by me.

Mom did let me have the hardwood in my bedroom. But my hopes were dashed while checking on the result, when I discovered that each step across my floor produced a loud, hollow ache. My floor was nothing like the sturdy hardwood floors of the ranch. I had made a miserable choice. I sat in the middle of the room and cried.

"Let's go shopping, shall, we?" It was Mom's voice and her words were loud, drowning out my sobs. "Maybe we could get you a big rug?" She made it feel like Christmas and we spent the evening staring at rugs and bedroom sets and dinnerware and Mom eased the pain of it all by purchasing everything we wanted. The next day was moving day.

When we were finished loading our few boxes of clothes, records, and books into the rented moving van, I couldn't help but notice how cavernous the truck was. All that emptiness hit me hard and I tried not to let anyone see my face as I swiped at the tears. Mom handed me the keys to the truck. "You drive."

KK, Mom and I climbed into the cab and I started up the engine. I slowly drove down the driveway, past the camellia bushes where I had hidden as I watched the police officer bring my drunken father home; the juniper bush where I had fumbled miserably with my first kiss; and the crooked-top pine tree where I had hidden from Dad after I burned out his truck brakes.

I was shaking. It was easy to hate Dad and blame him for everything. But who was going to take care of him now? And Mom with her new-found freedom and self-centered righteousness. Wasn't she to blame? But she was only doing exactly as we had asked. Guilt poured in from some unseen lava flow and I knew I was angriest at myself. I was the one driving us away, our lives destroyed. But some small part of me was relieved. Happy even. I couldn't believe it. How could I have been excited as I sorted and packed and lifted? And now when it finally came time to leave, I just couldn't bear it. I suddenly remembered something important.

I looked into the massive side mirror, as my home retreated behind us, the porch getting smaller and smaller—this was all wrong. "We forgot the kitchen chairs!"

Mom was stiff as she turned to look at me, her hands balled into tight fists. "We'll leave them behind. We'll get new ones. Just drive."

"No! Those chairs are special. I want mine." I hadn't asked for much. I hadn't gotten to bring my bedroom furniture. I just wanted this one thing. My chair.

Mom pressed her lips together, shaking her head. Her words felt like bullets. "The new ones will be perfect. Just drive." It was her rare *Don't-mess-with-me* voice, and I didn't push it.

Back when I was in kindergarten, all five of us kids were living at home, and life was normal. Mom and Dad had purchased a large wooden kitchen table and matching chairs—and they had decided to personalize each chair, with Mom sketching out our names and personalized images on each seat, and Dad burning those images into the wood with a tool that looked like a pen. I can still recall the thrill I got at the smell of the wood burning, small puffs of smoke rising into the kitchen, as the wild galloping horse emerged onto my chair. I remember standing too close and being shooed away, but later sneaking back into the kitchen to touch the dark burn scar in the wood, still warm from Dad's efforts.

KK's and Walt's were musically themed. My brother Don's was all about baseball. Sister Margery's chair had the phrase "Please sit down," in French—as well as a stage and curtain. Mom's had a remarkable likeness of herself singing, and Dad's had a naval ship, a destroyer to be specific, moving out on the ocean. His chair was at the head of the table, the only one with arms. I could hardly contain myself as we all sat down at dinnertime—each of us in our very own chair!

Now as I sat in the vacuous moving truck, I imagined those chairs lined up around the table. And Dad there all alone, crying.

We tried to make our new home special. But at every turn of the head, I felt unmoored. Raking green shag carpeting, no orchard, shiny new everything reminding me of what we left behind—especially the new dark rattan kitchen table and chairs which would have been happier on a patio in Hawaii. But Mom just kept buying and buying, trying to fill the void.

When we got together with friends from the old neighborhood they'd tell us of the young couple—Mona Lisa and John—whom Dad brought home one day and then invited to stay. He bought them a forest green truck, in return for taking care of him.

As the summer months wore on, they held loud parties in our childhood home. I learned from my best friend Julie that her father had marched over to the house on Saturday night to ask my dad to turn down the volume on the stereo. Her father reported the place was a mess, but that Dad was gracious and turned down the music immediately. I sobbed at the news. How could life have gone so wrong? I missed my old bedroom and the garden, and that stereo.

And then the worst thing happened. Twice Dad tried to visit at the condo. It wasn't me he wanted to see, just KK. The first time it happened, his caretakers walked him to our front door. Then came three loud knocks on the door. "Karen! It's your dad. Come out here!" KK looked at me, eyes wide, shaking her head no. Suddenly I was her protector. I thought about saying something like, "She's not here" or, "She can't come to the door" but that sounded so stupid I decided silence was best. We hid in the closet of our new house, praying he'd leave.

A few weeks later early in the morning, Mona Lisa and John backed into our driveway because Dad could no longer walk. He was on an old mattress in the bed of the truck. From their parking space, Dad was able to look up at the balcony, where our bedrooms were. Had he known that's where we slept?

Dad began hollering as soon as the truck parked. "KK! Karen! Aw, KK. Come out and talk to your dad!"

KK sobbed on her bed while they sat in the driveway for nearly an hour. "C'mon—just a couple minutes of your time, Karen! I want to know how you're doing!"

In my adjoining room, I sat waiting for my name to be called. What would I do if he asked for me? I went to the balcony window and peeked through a slot in the curtains. Had I wanted him to see me? Dad's belly was swollen—but at least he was dressed. I had to hand it to Mona Lisa and John. They took good care of him. I felt a deep stab of jealousy, for them and for KK. Why wouldn't he call out to me? What had I done?

CHAPTER FIFTEEN

Fearing Dad would show up again, I'd spend hours at the ballet studio each day, and I spent most nights and weekends at my grandparents' house. I had always felt safe there. As a kid they'd mutter apologies about Dad's treatment of me. Grandma would pat my hand. Louie would slip me dollar and a wink. Small comforts, but tangible. I had taken a picture of them at my high school graduation, flanking Mom. The shadow of Dad's absence that day clouded their faces, but they stared straight into the lens, their eyes as dark as the Pacific.

Each time I arrived at their house Grandma would open the door, her grey pixie wig catawampus on her head, "Well, look what the cat brought in, Lou!" She'd pat me on the back, ushering me inside, as I softly brushed past her drooping breasts. Then she'd sniff the Kentucky Fried Chicken bucket I'd place in her arms. "And she brought dinner too!" I tried not to scrunch up my nose as I moved past her. She'd forgotten to bathe again; her ripe musty stink, hard to ignore.

After dinner, Grandpa Louie would start in on Mom. Everything including Dad's drinking was blamed on her. It wasn't fair. She had always been his darling daughter-in-law, she'd call them every morning. She was the one who made sure we all had Sunday dinner together every week, even when Dad didn't show up. And now, she had filed for divorce from Dad, and Grandpa Louie had banned her from his home.

I had planned to work on this problem by shedding some light onto what it was like to have Dad as a father. After all, I was the expert, wasn't I? But I didn't have the heart to go into detail. Dad was their son. Everything that came to my lips was too vile, too unbelievable. He'd sound like a monster. I didn't want to do this to them. I didn't want them to know the truth.

So I decided not to tell them. I'd just listen. Besides, I was upset with Mom too. I didn't want her to drop by either. It was hard to believe that she was the same woman who now dug in her heels and made a big deal out of everything. Six months after filing for divorce, she'd moved back to our hometown into a house perfect for her growing vocal studio. She had a boyfriend who lived there, and had doubled her number of students.

I felt forgotten. Now if I wanted to see her, she'd put up her index finger, the universal "wait-a-minute" signal, and reach for her red leather appointment book. I missed the old Mom. Sure, she had a bedroom for me, but it didn't feel right. Her face would get all twisty like she wished she could have more privacy. I needed to get out, to move on, but I wasn't sure how to do it.

One day I showed up at her door with a freshly lit cigarette dangling from my lips. I lifted and released the heavy doorknocker and heard it reverberate inside her home.

Mom opened the door with smile, clearly expecting someone else, her face falling as she took me in. One eyebrow arched. "What's that in your mouth?"

I shrugged. "A cigarette. . . no big deal." I took a deep drag and blew it out slowly, my eyes slits, as if I were a poet contemplating my next lines. A thin snake of smoke hung in the air, just like Dad's used to. I stifled a cough. I wanted to gag. What was I doing?

"There will be no smoking in this house. Besides, I have a student arriving any moment." Mom placed her hand on her chest, just above her décolletage, her fingers fanning out like a shield, pressing into her flesh. Was she protecting herself from me? Her thick gold bracelet glinted in the sun.

I nodded. "Guess I better be going then." I spun on my heels.

My sudden movement surprised her, or maybe she felt guilty. "Honey?"

I crushed the cigarette into the driveway and sped off, unable to hear her next words. What was I doing? Had I really expected her to drop everything to hang out with me? And what's with the cigarette? I had just forced some nauseous memory of Dad back into my head, and maybe her head too. I wasn't this person. I didn't want to be this person.

As I mindlessly drove, I thought about all the changes that had happened that since Christmas: Mom's decision to leave and Dad's tears; me driving the moving truck away from everything I loved; Dad's drunken visits to the condo and KK refusing to talk to him; Mom filing for divorce and then falling in love. And all the while I dangled like a kitten by the scruff of my neck, with no control over what happened next. What would it take for me to get free?

I thought about friends off at college—they were following some path that made sense. Why couldn't I? I was good at school, sometimes a serious student if I was really interested in the subject, but lately I just couldn't get into anything. I was 19. I needed a life—just not mine.

Maybe I needed to have fun. I laughed at this thought. I couldn't even do that. Relaxation, time off, vacation—whatever you called it, it wasn't for me. Fun was for those who didn't want to get their hands dirty or do the job well. It was for sissies with no work ethic. *Oh God, Dad's voice again.* His voice was persistent, chanting words in my head. *Stop it! Leave me alone!* I pulled over onto the side of the road, my face sopping wet.

The next day I lingered in bed, listening to the mourning doves calling from the telephone pole. I felt lighter, as if yesterday's tears had elevated me above the clouds. I needed a new start. I leaped out of bed with the seed of an idea, and called Mom.

"Good morning! You know how you've always said I was really handy?" I was too chipper for the hour.

"Yes. . . " Mom whispered into the phone.

"If I did a lot work around your property, could you help me with rent on a little place of my own?" I closed my eyes and imagined her expression. I had never asked to be paid for the things I did. I was always doing things for mom: spackling and painting walls, repairing furniture, or doing simple things like getting her VCR to stop blinking on and off. Would she be angry with me?

I heard her place her palm over the phone receiver, followed by a muffled conversation. Two voices. I shivered as I realized she was repeating my offer to her boyfriend. He was probably in the bed with her at this very moment. Even worse, I probably woke them up. Mom popped back on the line. "Just a minute honey." She sounded groggy, not angry. I crossed my fingers.

Mom didn't have much power, but she did have money. Her inheritance came from booze, having been born into a family who owned a brewery, and had run beer during Prohibition. It always made Dad laugh that Mom's high and mighty privilege in society was entirely due to alcohol. He was known to holler out to her as we climbed into the car for church, "I wonder what the church would think if they knew where the source of your donations came from?" It felt like a threat, but Mom would shake her head, a dismissive I-can't-hear-you expression on her face.

Mom had tried to offer up her inheritance for Dad to pay the mortgage on the house, but he refused, saying, "Your money is your money. Don't want to see a dime of it." So Mom had decided to use her trust fund checks to do things Dad refused to pay for: piano and ballet lessons for us; opera and symphony tickets; large donations to the church and the civil rights movement. And then there were the shopping trips in the City. It took me years to realize those trips always happened shortly after Dad had done something "unfortunate" like totaling Mom's car and walking home as if nothing happened; telling me to sample sulfur dioxide-laced apricots to prove they were safe; forcing KK and me (due to our small size) to install asbestos-coated insulation in the garage attic after discovering it caused cancer; standing up blind drunk and singing the "Toreador" aria from the opera *Carmen* at the top of his voice to the entire restaurant on Mom's birthday.

Mom may not have protected us as a normal mother would have, but we soon came to count on her to use money to soften Dad's blows. It was a comfort we began to expect.

Mom's voice suddenly came over the telephone as I sat on my bed staring out the window. Her words were glittering into my ear. "Clever idea! I'm certain I could work something out. When would you move out?" That last line sounded like something her boyfriend would say. Once again, I was struck by how much Mom had changed.

———

I began looking for a place to rent. I found a small house in Santa Cruz along the river then bought a Quarter horse and horse trailer. In order to pay for my habit, I photographed and hauled horses for a living, and when that didn't bring in enough money I bartered for my stable fees by mucking out stalls and doing labor.

I loved working my body hard. Physical labor helped me clear my head: I'd hauled bales of hay from one end of the barn to the other, shoveled manure, chopped cords of wood for winter then stacked them. I'd be so depleted by the end of the day I had little time to even think. At night I'd lay down on the bed, images floating behind my eyelids: brief flashes of Dad's toothless grin, my hand immersed in steaming water, and blood dripping from my nose. The nightmares had begun. Then I'd get up and do it all over again the next day.

A month later, KK moved in with me. Although we never talked about Dad, I knew he was on her mind too. As we got closer, sharing dinners and music, I wondered how different her memories were from mine. KK was Dad's "favorite" but there was something that made her wither when we talked about him, something that lingered in the air.

But she never brought it up. Each night I'd sit exhausted in front of the TV with KK, watching the news. Endless accounts of Watergate, secret tapes, stories of President Nixon's possible impeachment flashing on the screen. We'd yell back at the news, outraged with the older generation. What was happening to America? It made me even more grateful for my work at the barn. At least when I was near the horses and working hard, I was in control.

One day, our sister Margery called. "Dad's back in detox. You've got to go see him."

"Oh. . . " The memory of that place engulfed me like a black cloud—the smells and shouts of the men. My shaking body, unable to enter his room.

KK narrowed her eyes as I listened to our sister. I mouthed Margery's words, and KK shook her head "no."

Margery was still talking, her voice cranked up a notch.

I wondered what I had missed. She spat out, "You'll never forgive yourself if you don't go. I mean it."

"I heard you. I just don't know what to do."

KK whispered, "You don't have to do what she says."

Margery was now loud enough for both of us to hear. "Go see him for God's sake. Say goodbye. I just visited and it wasn't that bad." A tone of worry crept into her last words. "He did think there were snakes all over his body."

An involuntary groan came from my mouth. He had imagined snakes writhing all over his body when I'd been there too. I shook the image from my head.

"Okay, I'll go." I looked at KK and lifted one shoulder, my apology for the lie.

Margery exhaled. "Good. If you don't, I swear it will haunt you for the rest of your life."

I'd never told anyone about my failed attempt to see Dad. Never admitted to being unable to even walk through the doorway into his room, to stand by his bedside. If I did would Margery stop pushing us to visit him?

I thought about her last words, ". . . it will haunt you for the rest of your life."

Margery was wrong. What haunts me is a father who never once held my hand or hugged me goodnight. A father who never noticed that I loved the things he loved: horses and the land; freedom to be alone; the open sky and mountains; granite lakes and forests; a broken-in pair of boots. I thought back to the last time I heard his voice when he called out from the driveway, repeating KK's name over and over as she cried. I'd sat there like an obedient little girl waiting for him to call *my* name. No, this is what haunts me: the fact that something about me pained him so deeply he'd prefer to look the other way; to pretend I didn't exist.

When I hung up I thought about Dad's caretakers, Mona Lisa and John, the perfect couple. I imagined them visiting him every day at the hospital, feeding him like a baby, stroking his hair or telling funny stories, maybe even smuggling him a drink now that the end was near. They were his model children—caring for him and never complaining. I hated them now more than ever.

The phone rang early the next morning. I leaped out of bed, my stomach already a tangled mess. Images spun in my head: my horse lying on the floor of his stall, the vet shaking his head. I fumbled with the phone nearly knocking it off the table.

"Honey?" Mom's groggy voice surprised me. It had been weeks since we had spoken. She never got up this early.

"Mom?" The wind howled, scraping a branch against the window. I shivered in my nightgown and grabbed the old Indian blanket off the couch, wrapping it over my shoulders, as if protecting me from what she was about to say.

She said it in a rush, too fast for the message. "Your father passed away this morning, honey." The white-hot words stung as I clutched the edge of the bookcase and sank to the floor. Had I heard her correctly? I had been so certain he was indestructible. How had it come to this? Was it my fault? How many times had I wished he'd die? I curled into a ball on the floor, the phone pressed to my ear. Dad had just turned fifty-four.

I heard myself ask, "Will we have a funeral?" While we were no longer an intact family, certainly this is something we must do. He was still our father and her husband. This was the right thing to do, wasn't it? I knew Christian Scientists didn't believe in death, or holding funerals but Mom certainly had attended a lot of them. I thought perhaps she'd consider a memorial service. "Mom? Will we?"

I must have said something to set her off, because her

voice felt like a knife cutting me loose. "Tell your sister. I've got to go." Dial tone. *What just happened?*

Had she just hung up on me? The old Mom would never have done that. The old mom would have said I'm sorry and lingered on the phone. This new mother, with her stupid boyfriend and busy studio with more-important-than-me students made me want to scream.

Why hadn't she answered my question? If I ever had children, I would always answer their questions. The truth would fly from my mouth until they had heard it all. I suddenly had to get out of there. It was an urge so strong, like an ancient instinct rising up, clutching my throat. *Get out!* I needed the smell of the forest and the warmth of my old saddle and the sound of Beckett's breath to clear my head. I needed this one thing. Just this one thing.

I wrote a note, taping it to KK's bedroom door—*Dad died. Don't hate me. I have to go riding.* It looked shameful stuck there, like a grocery list. I should have woken her up, I should have cried with her, but I stuck it there because I told myself I had to: because she was a late sleeper; because I couldn't stand being the one to say the words aloud; because like Dad, I'd much prefer to escape into nature, to be with animals and trees—the things that didn't talk back; because I didn't want to talk about what was going to happen next.

I slapped a sandwich together and dashed to the Jeep. I'd eat on the trail. Switching on the radio, the news blared. President Ford was pardoning President Nixon. I rolled my eyes. Then came the story that the FBI was putting up 'wanted' posters of Patty Hearst in all United States post offices. Jesus. Could the world get any weirder? I stuck the John Denver cassette tape into the stereo, put the Jeep into gear, and tore up the mountain, the cold air pushing past the gaps where the soft-top's plastic doors jangled against the body of the Jeep. Shivering, I pushed the heat lever all the way up.

On our ride, Beckett and I got lost, or more accurately, I did. Like all horses, Beckett knew exactly where he was in relation to home. I didn't. Together we explored switchbacks, dry creek beds, and clearings. We came upon old fences and abandoned homes I didn't even know were out there. Everything we saw was worth exploring. It drew me in, deeper and deeper into the mountain's beauty.

The ride helped me thaw from the morning's shock: The color of the leaves as they lost their chlorophyll and began to fade; the warmth of the saddle leather; Beckett's unwavering patience with my decisions to go this way or that. It all worked to calm my thoughts, to bring me back to myself. To help me feel.

But as I relaxed, memories swirled in the void, like dark smoke in a forest fire. Images of Dad's mocking smile; his cigarette bobbing as he spoke, his hand reaching for my face to teach me a lesson; his taunting voice urging me to trust him as I looked into the simmering pot of water; his glance at my reaction after the gun's explosion as my heifer's legs collapsed; his laughter at my unwavering obedience. I tried to clear my head. I tried to think of something else, but the past blackened my vision until I saw nothing else.

An hour later, I came to, my body rocking with Beckett's gait as he quickly climbed a hill. Clenching my jaw, I didn't recognize anything. Where were we? Guilt pumped though my veins. Shame on me for not protecting Beckett. Hadn't mountain lions been sighted here recently? Why had I let myself be consumed by the past? Beckett had been the only responsible one on the trail. I gave him his head. I loosened the reins as he descended hills and moved through the forest—eventually taking us all the way back to the stable.

When I returned home, it was almost dark. The note I had left for KK had been replaced by one from her. She was at our grandparents' home making Dad's funeral plans with Margery. Before I even took off my boots, I called them.

KK whispered into the phone, "Ariel's here—helping with arrangements." My breath caught.

Dad's sister lived in Southern California. She disapproved of our upbringing, especially of Mom, or at least that's what it felt like. KK was still talking, "She's saying that since Mom filed for divorce, it's not Mom's place to make Dad's funeral arrangements.

"You're kidding." I shook my head at the insanity of it.

"No, not kidding. . . and Mona Lisa and John arrived with Rebel, and he leaped out of their truck bed and went bounding all around the house, like he was a one-dog search party, really pissing Ariel off." I thought about Dad's big German shepherd cross, his wild wolf eyes and strong muscles. God, I missed his face. He had probably been searching for Dad. "Anyway, just a warning—Ariel says she's handling everything."

"What?!" I sat down hard on a kitchen chair.

In the background, Ariel's voice rose to shrill, "Are you meaning to tell me that. . . ?"

KK whispered, "Gotta go—Margery just suggested someone read some of Dad's favorite poems instead of having a pastor." The line went dead and I wanted to strangle my aunt.

Several hours later when KK came home, I handed her a cup of tea and our conversation continued at the kitchen table. "Ariel's insisting that Dad be dressed in a suit, but I explained that Dad would come back to haunt us if we allowed her to do that."

"You said that?" I smiled at KK's nerve.

She shrugged. "In the end she agreed on jeans, a shirt and his boots. It's going to be a closed casket anyway, so nobody will see him. That's the reason she agreed to it."

"What about flowers?" I was thinking about how Dad hated funeral flowers.

"I forgot that part. She couldn't believe it when I said Dad wouldn't want any flowers there. That he preferred them in the ground. In her world though, the more flower displays you have near the casket, the more love there is." KK thunked her cup onto the table and sighed. "Ariel kept shaking her head, saying things like 'Why must you kick convention in the teeth?' and, 'If you were decent children you'd want what's best for your father.'

"Jesus, I'm sorry I wasn't there to help." But I wasn't sorry, and KK knew it. I was an awful sister.

On the day of the funeral I arrived at the mortuary far too early and parked my Jeep next to a fleet of black hearses, glossy in the sun. I waited until Roberta Flack finished "Killing Me Softly," then switched off the radio. I leaned back into my seat, surrounded by the sudden silence. Did I really have to get out of the Jeep and walk inside? What if I didn't?

Having no black dress, I had pieced together the conservative outfit that Margery had suggested. Maybe she worried I'd show up in jeans and cowboy boots. I had thought about it, but I knew I'd get too much attention. I'd stick out. I didn't want to be seen, let alone interact with anybody.

Margery had warned me that people would probably say weird things in an attempt to help: *Time heals all wounds*; *After the storm the sun will shine; God never gives us more than we can bear.* "Just smile and say thank you, no matter what comes out of their mouths." I wasn't sure I could.

When I saw Mom's car pull up, I reached for my door handle and then realized she had arrived with her boyfriend. What was the hell she thinking? She was still married to Dad.

I worried about what my grandpa would do when he saw them together. I had to get to Grandpa Louie first. My head was throbbing.

As Mom emerged from the car, I could tell she had spent a great deal of time on her appearance: her royal purple boucle suit and the pearls Dad had given her long ago; perfectly coiffed hair; her mother's never-to-be-removed gold bracelet and her new engagement ring. Together they walked arm in arm toward the entrance to the mortuary, occasionally stealing glances at each other, as if they were walking down the aisle to get married. I wanted to scream, to tell her he didn't belong here. As they entered the building, KK's car pulled up and I dashed over to her.

"Mom brought *him* along," I muttered after we hugged.

"Oh, Jesus." KK craned her neck looking for Mom as we walked into the lobby of the mortuary. The first movement of Beethoven's Third Symphony played from the speaker. It was beautiful and strange to feel its power here. I needed a tissue.

As we entered the sanctuary I drew in a surprised breath at the sight of the pretentious casket: a highly polished dark wood that bore no resemblance to real wood, the very opposite of what Dad would have wanted. On top of the casket were hundreds of carnations, every one of them tinged with a pastel color, like Dad had been a sweet little girl. *Oh my God.*

I looked down at my feet, refusing to look at the flowers. I wanted to march up there and push those carnations off.

Carnations had always made me nauseous. I covered my nose at the stink of so many of them in this confined place and thought back to a summer day not so very long ago when Dad had done a science experiment on a tiny bouquet of unsuspecting white carnations that one of Mom's students had brought her. Dad had smirked as he squeezed five drops of blue food coloring into the vase while the student sang "Summertime," and by dinner that evening, all the carnations had turned powder blue. I called it magic, but Dad called it capillary action. Maybe the flowers were Dad's last laugh after all.

I sat down in the front row, on Mom's right, still plugging my nose. KK should have taken the chair on Mom's left, but Mom's boyfriend was already there, smoothing down his maroon leisure suit. KK plopped down next to me. Our aunt sat on the other side of her and began to pat KK's knee, reassuring her that everything was just swell. KK closed her eyes.

A man in a grey suit came out of nowhere and stood right next to the casket. Crisp and clean, a professional with a mask of sadness on his lips. "Dear family and friends. Thank you for coming today to honor the life. . . " (Here his eyes darted upward.) ". . . of Mack Donald Erickson."

Who was this guy? As if reading my thoughts, KK whispered, "That's the minister Ariel hired. She told me Dad was raised a Christian, and by golly he would be buried like one." I wanted to smack my aunt for this humiliation. For pretending Dad was someone he wasn't. For forcing us to pretend, too.

Her funeral plans made her feel better after ignoring her brother and us all these years—but this man's words were hollow. He didn't know Dad at all. We should have insisted on photos of the Sierras near the casket: close-ups of favorite horses; cattle lounging under spreading oaks; old Sid grinning next to a dusty pack mule; fishing for our dinners in an alpine lake; Dad at the Kit Carson parade in his flannel shirt, frayed jeans, and boots, his smile a mile wide as he gripped his gold-pan and blue ribbon.

Margery's husband Bob got up and I wanted to cheer. He'd save the day. Bob cleared his throat and his campfire-story voice warmed the crowd. He looked at us and said, "Kids, I was asked to read one of your father's favorite poems by Robert Service, set during a time in history I bet your dad wished he could have experienced: The Gold Rush. I certainly hope I can do it justice." I smiled at Bob's unassuming manner. A well-loved professor, he had entertained us—and hundreds of college students with his dramatic readings. I smiled to myself, certain what he was about to read. How would people react?

"There are strange things done in the midnight sun
By the men who moil for gold;
The Arctic trails have their secret tales
That would make your blood run cold;
The Northern Lights have seen queer sights,
But the queerest they ever did see
Was that night on the marge of Lake Lebarge
I cremated Sam McGee."

Aunt Ariel's face crumpled. She twisted around, glaring at us. Then I heard a sniff and looked over at Mom. She was searching for a tissue. As she wiped her face, I narrowed my eyes. Why the hell was she crying? She's the one who had filed for divorce. She's the one who was getting married to Mr. Leisure Suit next month.

"You're crying?" I whispered, when the poem came to an end.

"For what might have been, honey. . . for who he used to be." Mom dabbed at her nose, as I sat there realizing I had never known that good Dad. I was desperate to yell at everything around me: for being born too late; for the failure of this family to stay together; for me longing for its demise.

I buried my face in my hands, and KK put her palm on my shoulder and whispered, "Just remember, he can't get us anymore." My breath caught. She was right. It was over. I could put it all behind me. Then why did I still feel tense—as if Dad were watching my every move?

The funeral came to a close and our whole row stood up, wobbly. I didn't want to be hugged or spoken to. I didn't want to have to hear anyone's sage advice. I wanted out. Familiar panic seized my throat and my eyes darted toward the side door. Placing a hand over my stomach, I whispered into Mom's ear, "I've got to leave." I turned toward the door, my hand already reaching for the handle. As I slipped out into the parking lot, Margery called to me as she emerged into the sunshine, her disappointment at my sudden behavior, palpable. "You're not coming to the burial?"

"I can't. . . " I shook my head and made for the Jeep, peeling off the black sweater as I climbed in.

As I pulled out onto Highway 17 and headed into the Santa Cruz Mountains, KK's words, "He can't get us anymore," played a loop in my head. How could it all be over, just like that?

Part of me wanted to turn around and follow them to the cemetery, unseen and alone with my thoughts. I'd drive hidden from view for two hours to the little burial ground in Pine Grove that had loomed above old Highway 88 for the last two hundred years, home to gold miners, gunslingers, settlers and ranchers. Big dreamers, all of them, just like Dad.

Along the snaking country road, I'd pass the homemade fudge stand where two middle-aged sisters who never spoke made the best chocolate for miles around; and the hardware store, each aisle a goldmine, where I'd ride my horse to pick something up for Dad. Was I crazy for wanting to see it all again? But I couldn't bear the thought of what was waiting at the end of the journey—my ragtag family standing together on that dry oak-covered hill while that minister said words to gentrify the scene. No. I would not follow them into the Sierras. I pressed the accelerator for the stables in the opposite direction, in the Santa Cruz Mountains above the Pacific Ocean.

Midway to Santa Cruz, I took the Summit Road cut-off to the old two-lane road, the back-way to the stables, the one my grandfather used to drive before state Highway 17 was even thought of. As a passenger, the winding road made me nauseous. But as the driver, I was lost to my thoughts, peeling off layer after layer of the day: the imposing casket with Dad inside; the reek of carnations; Mom's tears; the stale stink of the mortuary; my aunt's shocked face; all the words left unsaid.

Gravel complained under the crush of tires as I pulled up the lane and saw the massive barn ahead. I stepped out to the familiar whinnies, but saw no humans. I passed the new Morgan mare and her dark little filly, clucked to old Pops, the massive draft horse, and stroked the muzzle of Charlotte, the aging blind mare who had a goat for a friend. It bleated as I passed.

Beckett spied me through the stall door. He offered me his low throaty nicker, more like a contented chuckle than anything else, and it pulled me closer. I grabbed the green halter and lead rope off the wall and slipped into his stall. "Hey Mr. Beckett." I stroked his face, making sure to rub between his ears—something he'd always bob his head for when I arrived, wrapped my arms around his neck, and buried my face in his soft coat. He smelled like hay and honey. Memories of all the horses I had ever loved came rushing though me. Beckett stood there unmoving, except for his whiskery chin, quivering as if he had something to say.

We rode into the hills to the smell of wood smoke as leaves shook in the breeze. Riding around a bend I came upon an old house, its front door weathered. I heard children giggling and imagined a pot of soup on the stove, a family safe and warm inside. We rode on, the weathered reins in my hand like a talisman, reminding me of all that had come before. This time, as the light began to dim and the sky carpeted in clouds, I was the one who caught sight of familiar territory and led us back home. Dad's body had been lowered into the grave in the mountains he loved more than gold. He was at peace. I wondered if I ever would be.

Vanya—a year after Dad's death

Mom and Dad on their honeymoon

Mack Erickson (right) winner of the 1963 Kit Carson Parade
"best costume" award

Vanya (age eleven) near the big oak tree

READING GROUP DISCUSSION QUESTIONS

1. Which scene was the most memorable for you? Why?

2. Share a favorite quote. Why did this stand out?

3. What feelings does the cover image of *Boot Language* evoke? Do you think it accurately hints at the story inside?

4. The first chapter opens with the protagonist as a newborn, bleeding as her mother prays. Why do you think Erickson chose to start there?

5. Which aspects of the protagonist's character do you identify with? Did any make you uncomfortable? Why?

6. Which character in *Boot Language* would you most like to meet? Why?

7. Discuss the traditional gender roles in *Boot Language*. Would this have been a different story if Erickson had been born a boy?

8. Discuss the tone of the book. How did the pairing of beauty and pain affect your reading?

9. The protagonist is outraged that her father plans to slaughter her pet heifer, yet she stands rooted to the action, determined to watch him do it. What does this reveal about her internal conflict?

10. At Thanksgiving dinner, Erickson's drunken father reenacts the aftermath of a kamikaze attack aboard his ship during WWII. How does this scene shift the protagonist's understanding of her father?

11. The protagonist cuts school to go see her father in the detox ward yet refuses to go to his bedside once she arrives. What conflicting forces inside make her behave this way? Ultimately, do you think she is glad she went to see her father? Why or why not?

12. As the protagonist drives the moving truck away from her childhood home, leaving most of the furniture behind, she asks to go back and retrieve her favorite chair. Her mother tells her to keep driving and she backs down, dropping the request. What is the significance of that decision?

13. This is a story about the relationship between the protagonist and her parents. Which character traits do you think she adopted from each of them?

14. *Boot Language* takes place in the 1960s and early '70s. How do you think the era impacts the way the story rolls out?

15. Do you believe Erickson's claim that she loves her parents? Is it possible to love someone who has harmed you?

ACKNOWLEDGMENTS

A million thanks to Carolyn Atkinson and Laura Davis for their wisdom and guidance; to my wild posse of writers: Autumn Vandiver, Cathy Krizik, Christine Holstrom, Claire Lovell, Danilyn Rutherford, Debbie Bates, Eileen Tejada, Gavriella Delgado, Jennifer Astone, Larae Ross, Magali Morales, Marie Hanson, Marlene Bumgarner, Mary Ashley, Melinda Iuster, Nancy Brown, Paldrom Collins, Rachel Michelberg, Renee Winter, Robin Somers, Sheila Coonerty, Susan Burrowes, Tony de Zompo, and Veronica Robinson; to Brooke Warner and She Writes Press for loving my story and putting it out there; and finally to my sweetheart, Henry Salameh, who listened and read and made a point of making me laugh every single day.

ABOUT THE AUTHOR

Vanya Erickson used to photograph and haul horses for a living. For the last 25 years she has been teaching writing and public speaking, as well as mentoring teachers in the oldest, continuously used schoolhouse in California. She's an active volunteer with Hospice Santa Cruz where she helps patients write to their loved ones. Firmly believing everyone has a story to tell, she enjoys finding music to help jostle memories of her patients. She loves hiking the High Sierras and coastal redwood forests, as well as dramatically reading aloud to children. Vanya holds a BA in Comparative Literature as well as a Teaching Credential, both from the University of California at Santa Cruz. Her essays have appeared in a dozen literary journals and anthologies, and in the book, *The Magic of Memoir.* Find out more about Vanya at www.vanyaerickson.com.

Author photo © Devi Pride

SELECTED TITLES FROM SHE WRITES PRESS

She Writes Press is an independent publishing company founded to serve women writers everywhere. Visit us at www.shewritespress.com.

The Sportscaster's Daughter: A Memoir by Cindi Michael. $16.95, 978-1-63152-107-2. Despite being disowned by her father—sportscaster George Michael, said to be the man who inspired ESPN's SportsCenter—Cindi Michael manages financially and heals emotionally, ultimately finding confidence from within.

Fourteen: A Daughter's Memoir of Adventure, Sailing, and Survival by Leslie Johansen Nack. $16.95, 978-1-63152-941-2. A coming-of-age adventure story about a young girl who comes into her own power, fights back against abuse, becomes an accomplished sailor, and falls in love with the ocean and the natural world.

The Coconut Latitudes: Secrets, Storms, and Survival in the Caribbean by Rita Gardner. $16.95, 978-1-63152-901-6. A haunting, lyrical memoir about a dysfunctional family's experiences in a reality far from the envisioned Eden—and the terrible cost of keeping secrets.

Don't Call Me Mother: A Daughter's Journey from Abandonment to Forgiveness by Linda Joy Myers. $16.95, 978-1-938314-02 -5. Linda Joy Myers's story of how she transcended the prisons of her childhood by seeking—and offering—forgiveness for her family's sins.

Veronica's Grave: A Daughter's Memoir by Barbara Bracht Donsky. $16.95, 978-1-63152-074-7. A loss and coming-of-age story that follows young Barbara Bracht as she struggles to comprehend the sudden disappearance and death of her mother and cope with a blue-collar father intent upon erasing her mother's memory.

Raising Myself: A Memoir of Neglect, Shame, and Growing Up Too Soon by Beverly Engel. $16.95, 978-1-63152-367-0. A powerfully inspiring and unflinchingly honest story of how best-selling author and abuse recovery expert Beverly Engel made her way in the world—in spite of her mother's neglect and constant criticism, undergoing sexual abuse at nine, and being raped at twelve.